The Invisible
Safety Net

The Invisible Safety Net

Protecting the Nation's
Poor Children and Families

Janet M. Currie

PRINCETON UNIVERSITY PRESS

PRINCETON AND OXFORD

Copyright © 2006 by Princeton University Press

Published by Princeton University Press, 41 William Street, Princeton, New Jersey 08540

In the United Kingdom: Princeton University Press, 3 Market Place, Woodstock, Oxfordshire OX20 1SY

All Rights Reserved

Library of Congress Cataloging-in-Publication Data

Currie, Janet M.
  The invisible safety net : protecting the nation's poor children and families / Janet M. Currie.
    p. cm.
  Includes bibliographical references and index.
  ISBN-13: 978-0-691-12268-7 (cloth : alk. paper)
  ISBN-10: 0-691-12268-7 (cloth : alk. paper)
    1. Public welfare—United States.   2. Poor—Government policy—United States.
3. Poor families—Services for—United States.   4. Poor children—Services for—United
States.   5. Child welfare—United States.   6. United States—Social policy—1993–
I. Title.

HV95.C86 2006
362.5'56'0973—dc22   2005052167

British Library Cataloging-in-Publication Data is available

This book has been composed in Janson text with Helvetica Condensed Display

Printed on acid-free paper. ∞

pup.princeton.edu

Printed in the United States of America

10 9 8 7 6 5 4 3 2 1

Contents

Acknowledgments

This book has grown out of my research with many others over the past fifteen years. I am indebted to my collaborators Anna Aizer, Jayanta Bhattacharya, Marianne Bitler, David Blau, Jeffrey Grogger, Jonathan Gruber, Steven Haider, V. Joseph Hotz, Enrico Moretti, Mark Stabile, Duncan Thomas, and Aaron Yelowitz. I also thank my mentors, Orley Ashenfelter, David Card, James Poterba, and Finis Welch, for their support. Christina Paxson's invitation to visit Princeton's Center for Health and Well-Being in 2003/2004 provided the impetus and the resources that made it possible actually to sit down and write. Tim Sullivan helped me over many rough spots and made extremely useful comments on the draft. Alan Burke, Tina Huang, and three anonymous referees also read and commented on the manuscript, for which I am grateful. Most of all I thank my husband, W. Bentley MacLeod, for his enthusiasm for the project and for his unwavering confidence that I have something to say.

The Invisible
Safety Net

Introduction

In 1994, welfare caseloads reached a historic high of 5.1 million families, about 15 percent of all American households. Since then, the welfare rolls have been cut in half, partly as a result of the strong economy of the late 1990s, and partly as a result of radical welfare reform, which began in 1996, when the Clinton administration fulfilled a pledge to "end welfare as we know it." The administration eliminated Aid to Families with Dependent Children (AFDC), the main cash welfare program for poor women and children in the United States, which had given cash payments directly to eligible women to support them and their families, and replaced it with the Temporary Assistance for Needy Families (TANF) program—its very name underlining the transitory nature of the assistance. TANF limited women to a lifetime total of five years of support, toughened work requirements, and strengthened sanctions on women who did not comply. Under TANF, the poor are no longer "entitled" to state and federal cash assistance, and the federal government's commitment to match state spending on welfare caseloads ended.

TANF brought with it dire warnings of catastrophe. A widely cited report from the Urban Institute, a Washington policy think tank, predicted that welfare reform would push 1.1 million children into poverty.[1] Two high-ranking Clinton appointees, officials at the Department of Health and Human Services, resigned in protest when President Clinton signed the bill.[2] Marian Wright Edelman of the Children's Defense Fund wrote an open letter to President Clinton protesting, "It would be a great moral and practical wrong for you to sign any welfare 'reform' bill that will push millions of already poor children and families deeper into poverty."[3] Senator Daniel Patrick Moynihan argued in the Senate that [this] "is not 'welfare reform,' it is 'welfare repeal.' It is the first step in dismantling the social contract that has been in place in the United States since at least the 1930s."[4]

The anticipated disaster never materialized, but commentators continued to warn that we had staved off disaster only because of the buoyant economy. The picture, they contended, would be considerably less rosy when the inevitable downturn occurred. Yet even during the recession and "jobless recovery" of the past few years, the number of children in poverty has not dramatically increased.

One reason we avoided disaster is that, even before the reforms of the mid-1990s, cash welfare had been a decreasing part of the welfare system for many years. In 1996, many families receiving AFDC also received "in-kind" assistance—food assistance, housing assistance, free medical care, and subsidized child care—programs providing specific goods, often targeted directly to needy children. Discussions of "welfare" often ignore these non-cash programs, even though they account for the bulk of spending on low-income families. Other safety net programs, most notably the Earned Income Tax Credit (EITC), provide cash. The EITC underwent a dramatic expansion during the 1990s and now provides more cash to low-income families than does TANF.

These programs, which came into their own with the rise of TANF and the end of cash welfare, form a largely invisible but tremendously important social safety net, providing basic necessities to poor families. As Douglas Besharov, a conservative commentator at the Heritage Foundation, noted, "Only the expanded aid now available to low-income, working families . . . makes it worthwhile for them to leave welfare."[5] In his book about welfare reform, *American Dream*, Jason DeParle put it more colorfully, describing cash welfare as one leg of a three legged stool that welfare mothers relied on for support. Since cash welfare was only one leg, it could be replaced by work or by contributions from friends or relatives.[6] My argument is essentially, that there is a fourth leg to the stool—support from the EITC and non-cash programs. By 2002 only a small fraction of aid to families, less than 10 percent, took the form of cash welfare payments—only 5 million people were on TANF. In contrast, even allowing for considerable overlap in the rolls of individuals who participate in these programs, more than 30 million people participated in other safety net programs including the EITC, Medicaid, food and nutrition programs, housing assistance, and subsidized child care. (A complete listing of expenditures and caseloads for the programs discussed in this book is shown in appendix table 1.)

These programs are the focus of this book, which assesses and analyzes the importance and effectiveness of individual programs in supporting low-income families (especially children) and discusses how both to ensure their continued existence and improve their performance. As I argue throughout the book, evidence suggests that in-kind programs are more effective than cash at improving the welfare of poor children in specific domains. It should surprise no one that a program like Medicaid, which provides health insurance to poor children, is more effective in promoting the use of health care than a cash program that is not targeted at any particular outcome. And while I assess the programs individually, they act together, providing a broad-reaching and comprehensive net that especially protects young children in low-income families. This may seem a basic point, but understanding how the different strands of the net reinforce one another is exceedingly important, not only to get a sense of how the United States treats its poor but also to reinforce the idea that these programs act together and do constitute a system, one subject to dismantling. Pulling on one thread—say, the funding of one part of one program—is liable to start the unraveling of the whole tenuous system, unless we recognize the reality that these programs create something greater, in much the same way that a net is greater than the sum of its individual ropes.

Senator Moynihan's belief that replacing AFDC with TANF would create terrible and widespread hardship was wrong, but his prediction that TANF would prove the first step in the dismantling of the social welfare system may well turn out to be right. The invisible safety net is under attack, and is in danger of being unraveled, one strand at a time. Perhaps the passage of TANF made it inevitable that critical eyes would turn from cash welfare to other aspects of the system. In the Brother's Grimm story, Cinderella shone in comparison with her wicked stepsisters. Similarly, programs that provide food and child-care benefits directly to children looked good in comparison to welfare programs that made cash payments to their parents. Now that the "wicked stepsister" of direct cash payments has been greatly reduced in importance, this comparison has become less salient and attacks are increasingly focused on the in-kind safety net programs themselves.

The battle to end all welfare programs has three fronts. First, critics single out individual programs, disputing both their efficacy and how they are administered. I argue that a careful investigation of the evidence suggests that most in-kind safety net programs are remarkably effective in improving the lives of poor children. As I discuss, critics have alleged widespread fraud in virtually every safety net program, including EITC, Head Start, the National School Lunch Program, and WIC (the Supplemental Nutrition Program for Women, Infants, and Children). These allegations have been investigated and proven largely without foundation. That is, virtually anything you can think of in terms of fraud probably has happened at least once, but there is no evidence to support common charges of widespread gross abuses. Yet each time Congress discusses the funding of a safety net program, these allegations of fraud and abuse resurface.

The ballooning federal budget deficit poses a more subtle but very real second threat to safety net programs. If the deficit continues to grow, as it has in recent years, we will increasingly hear arguments that there is simply no money left for anti-poverty programs for children. In this new fiscal regime, enormous pressure will inevitably press on non-defense-related federal programs, potentially squeezing them out of existence. Safety net programs for children are particularly vulnerable because Congress must periodically re-authorize spending on them. Given current budgetary realities, supporters of safety net programs will have to fight hard for the programs' very survival.

A third line of attack argues that, like TANF, control of the re-maining safety net programs should be transferred wholesale to the states. This approach poses a subtler challenge to the safety net. It does not appear on its face to cut any program, and it satisfies the current push for "states' rights." The programs discussed in this book are all currently subject to federal guidelines even if they are administered at the state or local level. Many of the programs are "entitlements," which means that anyone who applies and meets the eligibility criteria must be given benefits. An alternative vision of the safety net—the block grant approach—would take the money set aside for federal programs and give each state a block grant of fed-eral funds. States would then be free to design their own programs and to spend their block grants more or less as they choose.

The issue of which level of government should be responsible for which functions has always been controversial. According to Woodrow Wilson, "The question of the relation of the States to the federal government is the cardinal question of our constitu-tional system. At every turn of our national development, we have been brought face to face with it, and no definition either of states-men or of judges has ever quieted or decided it."[7] Many people be-lieve that anti-poverty programs should be devolved to the states as a matter of "states' rights." The idea that government at the state level is "closer to the people," and therefore better, sometimes seems to be taken as a self-evident truth. Such arguments might seem more a matter for constitutional scholars than for policymak-ers, but there are at least three economic reasons why such devolu-tion could pose a severe threat to the safety net.

First, a major practical difficulty with making the states responsi-ble for anti-poverty programs is that most states cannot run budget deficits. Under existing federal safety net programs, more people become eligible and entitled to assistance when times are bad. This means that federal payments for safety net programs rise automatically in bad times (the federal government can, and famously does, run deficits, meaning that it has few practical short-term spending limits). In contrast, under a state block grant system, there is no guarantee that federal payments to states will respond to economic conditions. Once the federal government delivers the grant, states are on their own. If state revenues fall as need grows, which is likely during an economic downturn, there will be cutbacks in state-financed services.

This is precisely what we're currently seeing. An unprecedented economic boom accompanied the implementation of TANF in the mid-90s, and states were able to use part of their TANF block grants for other purposes such as child-care assistance, while still covering those who met TANF enrollment criteria. But in recent years, cash-strapped states have been forced to cut spending on social welfare programs, and the proposed federal budget for 2005 threatens to cut the block grants even further. The federal government has ignored state pleas to increase assistance to offset declining state revenues. The current crisis in social services in many states would have been even more severe without the stabilizing influence of other federally financed programs.

Whether a program is more efficiently run at the federal or at the state level is an empirical matter that is likely to depend on the characteristics of the individual program. For example, programs like highway building may withstand periodic cyclical cuts in state budgets at little cost. States can build highways in good times and refrain from building them in bad times. But temporary cutbacks in the Medicaid program during bad times could permanently harm vulnerable children in a way that cannot be easily made up when budgets improve. It is much easier to fill a pot-hole than to help a child whose untreated hearing problem has already led to schooling delays. Neglecting children is likely to have widespread social effects down the road; it's not something we neglect in bad times only to pick up when the economy picks up. Children are not a public works project.

A second, related problem is that there is a real danger that federal block grants would fail to keep pace with necessary increases in expenditures. For example, the rising costs of medical care make the Medicaid program (which provides health insurance to low-income women and children, elderly nursing-home patients, and the disabled) one of the fastest growing government programs. At the moment, this is a problem not only for states but also for the federal government because the federal government matches state Medicaid expenditures. The fact that the federal government matches their expenditures gives states an incentive to keep spending on health care. In contrast, if the programs were block-granted to the states, and indexed to the rate of inflation, states would find that the block grant covered less and less of their expenditures for indigent care over time. Medical costs have been growing faster than the rate of inflation for decades, and there is no sign that this trend is abating.

The third and most fundamental objection to the block grant approach is that it would abandon any pretext of a uniform national safety net for low-income children. If we truly believe that no American child should be malnourished, that all children should have access to necessary medical care, and that every child should have access to high-quality early care and education, then it makes sense for the federal government to specify minimum standards for these services and to make sure that even the poorest states have the resources to provide them. The federal concern with civil rights justified abrogation of the state "right" to run segregated schools and enforce Jim Crow laws. Similarly, a pressing federal interest demands that the government ensure at least a minimal set of basic services for all American children.

Public support for the safety net springs from a strong desire to help poor children and a belief that children should not suffer for the shortcomings of their parents. But until recently, few researchers asked whether welfare benefited children. Researchers instead focused on whether cash welfare affected the behavior of parents; their main concerns were whether women on welfare earned less, married less, or had more children. No one has ever specified exactly what specific benefits (if any) children were expected to gain from parental participation in cash welfare. In contrast, the safety net programs discussed in this book have clear goals: We give children food because we do not want them to be hungry, we give them medical care so that they will not be sick, we provide housing so that they will not be homeless, and we provide enriched early care and education in an effort to promote school readiness. The focus should not be on what level of government has the right to administer such programs, or on grinding any ideological ax, but on how we as a nation can help poor children most effectively.

This book first describes the key components of the safety net and demonstrates that these individual programs can and do make a difference in the lives of low-income children. Moreover, in-kind safety net programs such as Medicaid, WIC, and Head Start have large and lasting effects on child well-being. Hence, they have quietly served as a more effective answer to the problem of poverty than the cash programs people usually focus on. Here is a common-sense proposition: It is easier to benefit children by providing them directly with things that they need than by developing programs that attempt to benefit children indirectly by changing their parent's behavior. While welfare reform has been very successful at getting low-income women to work, there is little evidence that this has had much impact, positive or negative, on children. The effectiveness of these alternatives to cash welfare is the focus of much of the book.

The important question for policy, however, is where do we go from here. I'll return to some options in the conclusion, but it's worth discussing them briefly now, before we begin our tour of the individual programs. The first option is to dismantle existing federal programs and start over from scratch with new programs that are administered at the state level. This is the option people seem to have in mind when they propose taking money from federal programs and block-granting it to states. I argue that dismantling existing programs in favor of untried ones would not be sound public policy.

A second option is to keep the structure of existing federal programs as it is but to make incremental reforms to each program. The discussion in this book acknowledges and catalogs many valid criticisms of existing safety net programs, and addresses specific reforms with respect to each program. Incremental reform may be the best that we can hope for in the current political and economic environment. Incremental change based on careful research is not glamorous, but it is likely to be more productive than scrapping existing programs entirely in favor of new, unproven ones. Moreover, dismantling the existing safety net program-by-program would leave gaping holes in efforts to help low-income families, which might or might not be filled by new programs.

A third, more utopian option, would involve the integration of existing programs into a much more effective safety net. Piecemeal reform of existing programs would leave important big-picture issues unaddressed. For example, one of the largest holes in the current safety net is that it does not serve all eligibles. Individual programs all have different eligibility criteria and require different actions on the part of would-be users, greatly increasing the costs of participation to poor families. Even if a systemic reform is not likely to be adopted in the near future, it is useful to have a vision of what it might look like. The final chapter lays out this vision.

Briefly, I argue that coordinating eligibility requirements across programs would cut administrative costs and help poor people to access these programs. Integrating existing programs into a stronger safety net would also help to convince people to think about these programs as a whole—as strands in a single net—rather than as a series of unrelated individual programs. Attacks on the individual programs seldom make the front page because most readers don't see that the safety net comprises many programs and that tugging too hard on one strand of the net may lead to its unraveling. And since attacks tend to come in the form of Congressional discussion of the arcane rules and complicated funding arrangements that stand behind most of these programs, matters of vital importance to many families remain buried in obscurity.

An even more radical reform would involve using the tax system to administer the safety net, which is currently how the EITC works. This would allow the government to phase out slowly many different types of program benefits as recipients' incomes rose. At present, the fact that people stand to lose many benefits with slight increases in earnings is a disincentive to work, and a barrier to economic advancement.

Most other books about poverty and welfare reflect public and scholarly preoccupations with cash welfare programs and largely ignore this invisible safety net. Years of benign neglect by scholars and policy analysts pose their own threat to the safety net, as policymakers may not recognize the importance of key programs until it is too late. More than a decade of research has convinced me that safety net programs generally accomplish their goals and are a crucial part of the continuing fight against poverty among children. If we truly believe that our children are our future, then we must protect these programs against those who would dismantle them, and move forward with reforming them to face the twenty-first century.

Chapter 1

Welfare vs. "Making Work Pay"

Ronald Reagan hit a nerve with his story about a Cadillac-driving Chicago "Welfare Queen" who used 80 aliases, 30 addresses, a dozen social security cards, and four fictional dead husbands to defraud the government of $150,000. In truth, the woman he was referring to had used two aliases to collect $8,000 in overpayments, but the truth did not matter. The public was outraged because the story fit negative perceptions about welfare.[1]

A survey taken in the 1980s found that 41 percent of Americans thought that too much was being spent on welfare, and that only 25 percent thought that too little was spent. But when the words "assistance for the poor" were substituted for "welfare" in the same survey, 64 percent favored higher spending and only 11 percent said that we should be spending less. Americans wanted to help the poor, but did not believe that welfare did so.[2] It was not surprising, then, that President Clinton's famous promise to "end welfare as we know it" struck such a responsive chord.

The problem with welfare was that its two main goals were in fundamental conflict. The program aimed both to provide a decent standard of living to children and to encourage self-sufficiency among their parents. Cash payments to single mothers could eliminate child poverty, but given that a mother's benefits were reduced with every dollar that she earned, and that she was likely to be cut off altogether if she married, the program discouraged mothers from working and marrying. To get around this problem, lawmakers had targeted an increasing share of aid directly to children in the form of benefits such as medical insurance, nutrition assistance, public housing, and an array of smaller programs.

By 1990, only $18.5 billion, or 14.1 percent of the $131 billion that was spent on aid to families with children was spent on cash welfare payments, while only 15 years earlier, in 1975, the comparable figure had been 26.6 percent. Appendix table 1 shows in-kind aid program by program. Still, assistance from other programs was closely linked to receipt of welfare. As of 1990, virtually all children on welfare (Aid to Families with Dependent Children or AFDC) received food stamps and Medicaid, half of AFDC children received free school lunches, 35 percent lived in public housing or received rent subsidies, and 19 percent participated in WIC (the Supplemental Nutrition Program for Women, Infants, and Children). In 1984, a quarter of all single-parent families received AFDC, Medicaid, and food stamps, and an additional 11 percent received at least one benefit in addition to AFDC.[3]

The close connection between eligibility for welfare and eligibility for other programs severely penalized earners. In 1990, a mother with two children could increase her earnings from zero to $15,000, and only increase her actual "disposable income" by $587! The reason was that as her earnings increased, she would progressively lose not only her cash welfare benefits but also all of the other benefits that were tied to it. When her earnings hit $7,000, she would lose AFDC, and when her earnings hit $10,000, she would lose both food stamps and Medicaid. In the meantime, child care and other expenses would rise with earnings.[4] It is no wonder that commentators criticized the "welfare trap."

The seeds for changes in this system were sown well before the 1996 welfare reform bill, the Personal Responsibility and Work Reconciliation Act (PRWORA). First, it is worth repeating that only a small and declining share of aid to families with children was in the form of cash welfare payments prior to welfare reform. Second, the close link between receipt of welfare and eligibility for other programs had been loosened. Beginning in the 1980s, additional groups of women and children became eligible for free public health insurance as described further in chapter 2, and eligibility for other forms of aid, such as food stamps, had never been directly tied to welfare receipt.

Third, the early years of the Clinton administration saw a huge expansion of the EITC (Earned Income Tax Credit). The number of recipients grew from 12.5 million families in 1990 to 19.8 million in 2003, and the maximum credit grew from $953 to $4,204! The rapid expansion of this obscure program, run through the tax system, can be thought of as "stealth welfare reform" since it has resulted in cash transfers to low-income families that are larger than those that were available under either the old AFDC program or the new TANF (Temporary Assistance for Needy Families) program. Craig Gunderson and James Ziliak estimate that the EITC accounted for half of the reduction in after-tax poverty that occurred over the 1990s (the other half being mainly accounted for by strong economic growth).[5]

The EITC is a tax credit available to poor working families. Its essential feature is that it is "refundable"—in other words, a family whose credit exceeds their taxes receives the difference in cash (only this refundable part is shown in appendix table 1). Hence, the EITC is like welfare in that it gives cash payments to poor families; but it is fundamentally different than welfare, because it gives cash only to poor families that work: EITC recipients need to work and file tax returns to be eligible. The size of the payment increases with earnings up to a maximum level before being phased out, so that it gives the poorest households an incentive to work. The credit is set at a level high enough that a family with one earner working full-time at the minimum wage is raised above poverty.

This chapter first presents evidence about the effects of the old AFDC program on child well-being. It then discusses the transition to the new TANF program, and the rise of new cash assistance programs such as the EITC. I argue that cash payments of the size offered under the AFDC/TANF program cannot be expected to have much of an impact on child well-being. Hence, neither the old program nor the transition to the new program had much measurable effect on child outcomes. The EITC has had more dramatic effects, both on the way households function and on family incomes, though there is little evidence available about its effects on children. In-kind programs appear to have the largest measurable effects on child outcomes, perhaps because they are targeted toward specific outcomes.

The Old Welfare System

AFDC was created in 1935 to provide support for fatherless children. At the time it was created, most female heads of households were widowed, and widows were expected to stay home and care for their children. Hence, there was no conflict between providing income support and encouraging mothers to work. AFDC was an entitlement, which meant that in principle all children who met the eligibility requirements were entitled to support. In practice, however, before the civil rights movement began to challenge restrictive state practices, few African American children received support.

The program was run as a federal-state matching grant program, which meant that states set their own eligibility standards, and the federal government then matched state payments. This led to a huge amount of variation in benefits among states. For example, in January 1991, the maximum AFDC grant for a one-parent family of four varied from $124 a month in Alabama to $891 per month in Alaska. This variation is too large to be accounted for by differences in the cost of living between states, so that real levels of support varied widely. Except in the most generous states, benefits did not begin to approach the federal poverty line, which would have been $13,942 in annual income for a four-person family in 1991.

It is hardly surprising that this program did not eliminate poverty. Consider the choices facing an Alabama welfare mother receiving $1,488 per year under the old AFDC program. On welfare, she would have been thousands of dollars below the federal poverty line, which is the minimum amount the federal government believes families need for food, shelter, and other necessities. But if she increased her earnings (and reported them to her case worker) her welfare benefits would be docked almost dollar for dollar, and she would be at risk of losing automatic eligibility for many other benefits such as food stamps, public housing, and public health insurance.[6]

One might well ask how anyone could live on $1,488 per year? It would be extremely difficult even with assistance from other programs, so that cheating was virtually built into the system. Kathryn Edin and Laura Lein's book *Making Ends Meet* documented the ways in which women on welfare struggled to supplement their income by soliciting money from friends, family, and boyfriends, performing odd jobs, engaging in illegal activities, and even taking regular, unreported employment. They document the fact that virtually everyone cheated. The neighbors of the one mother who tried to live off her benefits were considering reporting her for neglect because her son went hungry so often. Edin and Lein's careful accounting for the budgets of these women suggest that very little was spent on items that were not absolutely essential, indicating that they literally could not get by without under the table earnings. One in eight mothers said they had kept their children home from school because they lacked winter clothing. The AFDC program was so unattractive that a third of eligible poor women did not even use it.[7]

Should we have expected this program to help children? There are two ways that it could have helped young children. The first is by increasing income. We know that on average, higher-income children do better than poor children on virtually every measure, though there is controversy about whether this reflects the effect of income per se, or the effect of other factors like parental skill that might be correlated both with higher income and better outcomes. The income available when children are young may be particularly important.[8] Under AFDC, the size of the income transfer to the average family was small (though it was larger in some high-benefit states). Moreover, given the work disincentives and marriage disincentives created by the program, it is not in fact obvious that welfare mothers had higher household incomes than they would have had if the program had not even existed.

Welfare could also have helped children by allowing their mothers to spend more time with them. As discussed earlier, however, if welfare mothers had to hustle to make ends meet, then it is not clear how much more time they would have had for their children, or whether that time would have been "quality time." Analyses of "welfare-to-work" programs have subsequently shed light on the question of whether making welfare mothers work hurts their children, as discussed later in more detail.

It is remarkably difficult to say whether welfare helps or hurts children. A simple approach would be to compare children on welfare to children who are not on welfare. Yet the children who are on welfare or who have been on welfare are almost always worse off than other children. This does not, however, mean that welfare has failed them. Without welfare, their situation might have been even worse. So the key question is, how well would these particular children have fared without welfare?

In work with Nancy Cole, I examined the effect of a mother's participation in AFDC during pregnancy on her baby's health. In simple statistical models that compared children of mothers with similar education and income, we found that welfare appeared to have *negative* effects on the baby's health! These negative results disappeared when we made a greater effort to compare the children of welfare mothers only to children whose mothers were similar. This example illustrates the fact that the children of welfare mothers are expected to have the worst outcomes on average, and that this may not have anything to do with a causal effect of welfare.[9]

Similarly, Phillip Levine and David Zimmerman showed that there were huge differences between children who spent time on welfare and those who did not: On a range of tests, the welfare children scored about two thirds of a standard deviation lower than the other children, which is a considerable difference (in these test score distributions, virtually all scores lie within two standard deviations of the mean score). Levine and Zimmerman also showed, however, that the welfare mothers had much lower test scores than other mothers. Mothers with low test scores themselves were both more likely to be on welfare and more likely to have children with low test scores. When Levine and Zimmerman took all of the characteristics of households into account, they found little difference between welfare children and others. So the differences in the children's test scores could not be blamed on participation in welfare.[10]

Welfare could actually have negative effects on older children, making them more likely to have teen pregnancies and/or to use welfare themselves. Conservative commentators like Charles Murray and Robert Rector believe that seeing their mothers use welfare lowers children's aspirations, reduces the stigma associated with welfare, and familiarizes children with the system. Using data from the 1980s, Peter Gottschalk showed that 29 percent of the daughters of welfare recipients ended up on welfare themselves, compared to only 12 percent of the daughters of non-recipient eligible mothers. Gottschalk speculated that this might be for the same reason that children of lawyers are more likely to become lawyers–familiarity with the profession makes choosing it more likely.[11]

In contrast, David Zimmerman and Phillip Levine argue that the correlation between mother and daughter's use of welfare could be entirely explained by the characteristics of the households where the AFDC daughters grew up, since both mother and daughter were likely to be poor.[12] That is, given that welfare failed to eradicate poverty, it should not be surprising that children of welfare mothers were more likely to end up poor and on welfare themselves.

One bright spot in an otherwise gloomy literature assessing the effects of AFDC, is a study by Jonathan Gruber. This study asked whether the program helped women who became single parents because of divorce. The majority of AFDC expenditures were on the stereotypical "welfare mother" who had never married, and who stayed on the program for a long time. Most welfare recipients, however, actually used the program for short periods of time in response to events—such as divorce—that suddenly reduced their income. Gruber focuses on this population of people who were using welfare as a short-term safety net. Although he does not directly look at the effects of AFDC on children, he does find that mothers who divorced and went on AFDC were able to maintain their consumption of food and housing.[13] For these mothers then, the program was supplying a safety net to tide them through temporary bad times.

Welfare Reform

The Personal Responsibility and Work Opportunity Reconciliation Act of 1996 put an end to AFDC and created TANF. PRWORA replaced the federal entitlement to welfare with block grants to the states. What this means is that when state funds for welfare dry up, eligible women and children can be turned away. PRWORA also established a five-year lifetime limit on welfare benefits, and mandated that recipients engage in work-related activities (mothers of children less than a year old may be exempted).[14] Aside from these provisions, the states gained new freedom to redesign their welfare programs.

The implementation of PRWORA was followed by dramatic declines in the welfare caseload. From 1996 to 2002, the caseload fell from 12,645,000 to 5,146,000 recipients. In percentage terms, the fraction of all U.S. children on TANF plummeted from 12.5 to 5.3 percent in only six years. Intense debate rages over whether all of these declines can be attributed to PRWORA, rather than to the unprecedented economic boom of the late 1990s. Conservatives would like to give PRWORA all the credit, while liberals would like to credit economic conditions. Studies that focus on these two factors find that 30 to 60 percent of the decline in welfare participation was due to PRWORA.[15]

Surprisingly, PRWORA seems to have had limited direct effect on the probability that a person worked while on welfare. Nominally, PRWORA required states to have 50 percent of their welfare caseloads in work activities by 2002. In fact, state work participation requirements were reduced if states were able to reduce their caseloads in other ways. Hence, in 2002, only eleven states were required to have more than 10 percent of their TANF caseload in work-related activities. Still, about 33 percent of TANF recipients were working in 2002. This means that many PRWORA recipients were working, even though they were not required to do so. These numbers point to other reasons for welfare recipients to enter the labor force.[16]

Several important studies indicate that the EITC (discussed later in more detail) reduced welfare participation by creating large incentives for poor single women to work. Hence, there is considerable evidence that carrots (plentiful jobs plus the availability of the EITC to those who worked) as well as sticks (forcing women to work or cutting them off from benefits) were responsible for the decline in welfare participation.[17]

Despite the dramatic declines in the caseload, relatively few women have actually run up against the five-year time limits. Instead of literally kicking people off welfare, PRWORA seems to have acted primarily by changing the climate in welfare offices. In her book *It Takes a Nation*, Rebecca Blank provides a vivid picture of welfare offices that were more concerned about "cutting checks" and the minutiae of eligibility criteria than they were about assisting mothers out of poverty. A recent study of bureaucratic practices in welfare offices indicates that caseworkers now place much more emphasis on getting mothers to work, and on using welfare as a last resort.[18] This change is reflected in many aspects of mother's behavior. For example, Jeffrey Grogger and Charles Michaelopoulos show that many poor mothers with young children now "bankroll" their five years of welfare eligibility, saving it for a rainy day.[19]

Aggregate post-PRWORA trends in employment and poverty among single mothers have been amazingly positive, at least relative to the apocalyptic scenarios that many commentators envisaged. The caseload decline was accompanied by a dramatic increase in employment among single mothers. The employment rate for single mothers with children under six went from 52.5 percent in 1995 to 67.5 percent in 2001. In 1995, these single mothers were less likely to work than married mothers, but by 2001, they were 8 percentage points more likely to work. At the same time, poverty rates for female-headed households fell, from 36.5 to 28.6 percent. For black and Hispanic families, the declines were even steeper: from 48.2 to 37.4 percent and from 52.8 to 37.8 percent, respectively.[20]

A more nuanced look at the data suggests though that some families were hurt by welfare reform. A study by the Center on Budget and Policy Priorities found that the average incomes of the poorest fifth of single mothers fell between 1995 to 1997, despite continuing economic growth. Marianne Bitler, Jonah Gelbach, and Hilary Hoynes look at different parts of the income distribution and find that while some women increased their earnings by a relatively large amount, others were not able to make up the lost income from welfare benefits and suffered declines in their income. At a more graphic and personal level, Jason DeParle's moving portrait of the impact of welfare reform on three poor, black women and their ten children ends with two of the women finding work that allows them to "just make it," while the third goes off the rails.[21]

Even if we focus on the women who have worked their way out of poverty, reasonable people could worry about the impact of welfare reform on children. The hope is that newly independent mothers will provide positive role models for their children. Yet, if mothers are working long hours, adequate child care is in short supply, and families are severely stressed by the new arrangements, children are likely to suffer. Still, a recent National Research Council report concludes that "no strong trends have emerged, either negative or positive, in indicators of parent well-being or child development across the years just preceding and following the implementation of PRWORA." DeParle calls the lack of any evidence for positive effects on kids the "biggest disappointment" of welfare reform.[22]

Perhaps the best evidence about the effects of welfare reform on children comes not from studies of PRWORA but from studies of changes many states made to their welfare programs in the years leading up to that national legislation. Welfare reform actually began in the early 1990s, as many states sought permission from the federal government to experiment with their welfare programs.

Experimental evaluations of a number of these "welfare to work" programs offer rich evidence about the potential effects of welfare on children. The best of these experimental studies worked just like a drug trial, in that they randomly assigned groups of women on welfare to "control" groups in which they received regular welfare, and to various "treatment" groups, where the treatments ranged from offering monetary work incentives to mandating that women participate in work or training activities.

In a drug trial, we can determine whether the new drug works by comparing the outcomes of the people who took the new drug with those of people who took a sugar pill "placebo." Since people are randomly assigned to the treatment and control (placebo) groups, on average there are no initial differences between the two groups, so that any differences that arise during the course of the trial can be ascribed to the treatment. Social experiments work the same way: If people are randomly assigned to treatment and control groups, then one can ascertain the effect of the treatment by simply comparing the mean outcomes of the two groups.

Studies of the welfare to work experiments conclude that some treatments actually had small positive effects on children, while others had small negative effects. In particular, treatments that resulted in increased household income were associated with small positive effects on cognitive and behavioral outcomes, even when the mother had to work.[23] On the other hand, treatments that reduced a mother's time with her children without increasing household income were sometimes associated with negative effects.

Several studies break out the effects that sending welfare mothers to work have on children of different ages. These studies come to the perhaps surprising conclusion that to the extent that they exist, negative effects are concentrated among adolescents. There do not appear to be any negative effects for younger children. Researchers speculate that when their mothers go to work, adolescents suffer both from reduced parental supervision and greater responsibility, especially if they have to look after younger siblings. One caveat is that there are few infants in the experimental studies. A growing body of research suggests that maternal employment may be bad for infants, especially in the first six months.[24] So it is possible that welfare-to-work initiatives that forced mothers of infants into the labor force would have harmful effects.

In summary, welfare reform appears to have had remarkably little overall impact on children. While many observers have been startled by this result, the literature offers an obvious explanation: If the old AFDC program did little for children, then perhaps one should not have expected abolishing it to have much impact either.

A second explanation is that much of the reduction in support through welfare has been made up by increases in support from other programs. James Ziliak looks at the fraction of the "poverty gap" that is filled by safety net programs. The poverty gap is defined as the difference between the poverty line and the average income of poor families. He finds that on average, anti-poverty programs filled a little more than 55 percent of the gap in 2001. This fraction is little changed since 1991. His definition is somewhat different than mine, in that he excludes Medicaid, child care, and nutrition programs other than food stamps. He also includes Unemployment Insurance and Worker's Compensation (while showing that these are of small and declining importance to poor families). If he had included the value of Medicaid and child care in these calculations, they might well have shown increases in the fraction of the poverty gap filled by the safety net.[25]

In some cases, families switched from welfare to other cash assistance programs. One of the programs that grew most rapidly was the Supplemental Security Income or SSI program, which assists low-income families with disabled members. To receive SSI payments, a person must have a disability recognized by the federal government, and must also meet income and asset tests. In May 2004, the average payment for an SSI child was $507.40 per month. Mark Duggan and Melissa Kearney calculate that for every 100 children who lost welfare between 1989 and 2001, 41 additional children received SSI payments. This increase occurred despite 1996 changes in the SSI program that made it more difficult for children to be categorized as disabled, and resulted in 100,000 children being thrown off the roles. Duggan and Kearney estimate that the overall increase in SSI participation reduced child poverty rates by 2 percentage points.[26]

The Growth of the EITC

A second cash program that has shown tremendous growth is the EITC. Welfare-to-work experiments suggest that children benefit when their mothers work if the mother's work raises family income. The EITC has had a dramatic impact on the incomes of many poor working mothers. Consider the case of Laura, a single mother of two school-age children.[27] Laura works thirty hours per week at Burger King at the federal minimum wage of $5.15 per hour. Over the year, her total earnings of $7,725 entitle her to an EITC of $3,090. Because of her low level of income, the size of the credit available to Laura increases by 40 cents for every dollar that she earns, so the EITC has the same impact as raising her hourly wage from $5.15 to $7.21 per hour![28]

Laura lives with her boyfriend of three years, Simon, who earns $24,000 a year in his job as a mechanic. Laura and Simon have discussed marriage, but they aren't sure they can afford it. If they marry, their combined income of $31,725 will make them all but ineligible for the EITC. The woman at H&R Block told Laura that if they marry, they will receive a credit of only $625 rather than the $3,090 she now receives. Neither Laura nor Simon have health insurance, and Laura worries that marriage would make her children ineligible for public health insurance under the Medicaid program. Laura would also lose her food stamps, and the kids would have to pay for their school lunches.

Simon argues that if they were to marry, it would make sense for Laura to quit her job and stay home. That way, the children would remain eligible for Medicaid, and an EITC of $2,252 would offset some of her lost earnings. Laura is not sure they could get by on Simon's earnings alone, and wants to retain some independence. Laura wants to increase her hours for a few years, so that she could get the maximum EITC credit of $4,204, and perhaps even put something aside for a rainy day. This simmering dispute about work and money is putting a strain on their relationship, and Laura sometimes wonders if Simon is the right person to be a new father to her children after all.

This story illustrates many important features of the EITC. First and foremost, it does provide significant help to many families, especially single mothers. Whether it "makes work pay" is debatable, but it certainly makes work pay more than it otherwise would. In 2003, 19.8 million families received an average credit of around $1,784. Eighty-nine percent of this money went to tax payers with income less than $30,000. The EITC raises many families above the poverty line (though perhaps we should not make too much of the difference between being a few dollars above or a few dollars below that level). For example, if Laura worked forty hours per week for fifty-two weeks per year, the credit would bump her income up to $14,916, which would be just above the federal poverty threshold for a family of three ($14,824). The EITC results in considerable increases in poor women's incomes, unlike traditional welfare, which trapped women in a Catch-22 situation in which they could not increase their earnings without reducing their benefits.

In contrast with welfare, which penalized women like Laura for working, the EITC rewards her by increasing her effective hourly earnings. It is not surprising then, that the EITC has resulted in dramatic increases in the employment of single mothers. Nada Eissa and Jeffrey Liebman were among the first to note that the EITC had important effects on the employment of single women. In an influential study, Bruce Meyer and Daniel Rosenbaum argue further that the EITC is the single most important factor explaining the increased employment of single mothers, and that it was much more important than welfare reform.[29] Jeffrey Grogger shows that the expansion of the EITC also raised the incomes of many women enough to prevent them from going onto welfare.[30]

There are however, several downsides to the EITC. The first is that it is administered through the tax system, which everyone loves to hate. Because it is part of the tax code, the EITC is complicated, and many poor families do not fully understand the provisions that apply to them. For example, one study found that though most families had heard of the EITC, most did not know that they needed to earn a certain amount in order to maximize their credit.[31]

These families often end up paying some of the credit to commercial tax preparers who advertise "instant cash back" or loans to low-income filers based on the size of the EITC credit that they will receive, and then keep some of the credit in payment for their services. In fact, Wojciech Kopczuk and Cristian Popl-Eleches show that participation in the EITC rose dramatically with the introduction of electronic filing, because it gave commercial tax preparers an incentive to court this market aggressively. On the positive side, perhaps because help from paid preparers is available, the take up of the EITC by eligible families has been high. John Karl Scholz estimates that over 80 percent of tax payers eligible for the credit receive it.[32]

There have been numerous reports of EITC fraud, though it is likely that many EITC errors are honest mistakes. For example, until 2002, the EITC used definitions of earned income and adjusted gross income that were different from the definitions of those concepts used on the rest of the tax form. Hence, simply transferring the number from the front of your 1040 form to the EITC form would cause an error. The most serious errors involve fathers filing claims for children who did not reside with them for at least six months of the year. In an effort to deal with this problem, the Internal Revenue Service has been using a new national child-support registry system since 2001 to see whether fathers who file for the EITC actually have custody of their children.[33] It is probably too early to tell whether these and other recent reforms have improved implementation of the EITC, but they are a step in the right direction.

The story of Laura and Simon illustrates a more fundamental problem with the EITC, which is that it imposes a "marriage penalty" on couples in which the woman earns much less than the man. There are many other examples of marriage penalties in the tax code. For example, the fact that the standard deduction for a married couple is less than twice the standard deduction for a single person means that many people will pay more if they file as a married couple than they would have if they had been allowed to file as single persons. The marriage penalty for low-income families like that of Laura and Simon, who benefit from the EITC, is compounded by their loss of other benefits as well as the EITC if they marry.

Still, the marriage penalty built into the EITC is especially pernicious given a growing consensus that single-parenthood is one of the leading causes of poverty among children. Single women are working more, but there is little evidence that women who move out of welfare and into work at low-wage jobs will see much growth in their earnings over time. If we want poor women to marry because we think that it will benefit their children, then surely we should not penalize them for doing so.[34] Ironically, the fact that more single mothers are working means that more women are potentially subject to EITC marriage penalties!

Some proposals to eliminate marriage penalties in the EITC would channel more of the money to higher-income households. For example, if joint filing were abolished, so that everyone filed separately, then all spouses with low incomes could file for the EITC regardless of their husband's earnings. Similarly, if married couples were allowed to split their income for EITC purposes, then Laura and Simon would be eligible for a credit of $3,755 if they married. This would, however, allow couples with incomes much higher than the current maximum of $34,692 to file for the EITC. For example, couples with incomes up to almost $70,000 would still be eligible.

A third option is to extend the "flat" range of the credit. The EITC rises with earnings at low levels of income, and then flattens out at the maximum credit ($4,204 for a family with two children in 2003) as income continues to rise. When earnings hit a threshold (which was $14,730 in 2003), the credit starts to phase out—it is reduced by 21.06 cents for every dollar earned. When earnings hit a maximum ($35,692 in 2003), the size of the credit falls to zero.

Increasing the flat part of the credit would reduce marriage penalties. For example, if the credit did not start to phase out until earnings hit $17,730, the size of the credit Laura and Simon would be eligible for, if married, would increase from $625 to $1,247. Families with incomes up to $37,692 would now be eligible for the credit, and so this measure also puts more of the money in the hands of slightly higher-income families, but the EITC remains much more firmly targeted at low-income families than it would be under the other proposals. Congress did in fact make a small change in the EITC along these lines in 2002, extending the flat part of the credit by $1,000 for married couples.

In addition to its legal complexity and its marriage penalty, a final problem is that the EITC could reduce wages at the bottom of the distribution by increasing the competition for low-wage jobs.[35] The intuition is simply that if more low-wage workers chase a fixed number of jobs, then wages in those jobs will fall. The size of this effect depends on how many people are drawn into the labor market by the EITC and on how the demand for workers responds. There are few reliable estimates of the size of this effect. Saul Hoffman and Laurence Seidman argue that it is likely to be small because while the EITC has drawn many single mothers into the labor market, these women are not a large share of all low-wage workers. To the extent that some married mothers have left the labor market as a result of the EITC, this will have an offsetting effect. On the other hand, the labor market remains highly segregated by gender (for instance, few construction workers are women, and few child-care workers are men), so it is possible that an influx of low-wage women into the labor market could have a relatively large impact on the wages of less-skilled women.[36]

Given that the EITC is targeted to families with children, it is surprising that there has not been any research examining the effects of the program on kids. The welfare-to-work experiments suggested that treatments that raised mothers' income had positive effects, and so one might expect the EITC also to have at least small positive effects. The only evidence on this point comes from a much older social experiment, "The Negative Income Tax Experiment," or NIT. Both the Carter and Nixon administrations proposed a NIT.[37] It specified a guaranteed minimum income for everyone. At low levels of income, the size of the benefit was to be reduced $.50 for each dollar of earned income, so that once a "breakeven" level of income was reached, the benefit fell to zero.

The NIT proposal differs from the EITC in that there is a benefit guarantee, so that even families without workers are supported. Under the EITC, only working families who file tax returns are supported. Moreover, under the NIT, any earnings are "taxed," while under the EITC, the size of the benefit first rises and then falls with earnings. But like the EITC, the NIT involved relatively large transfers to low-income families. While the NIT proposal went down to political defeat, large-scale experimental trials of the NIT were conducted in seven states between 1968 and 1982. In the trials, families received payments of between one-third and two-thirds the poverty line, so that in today's dollars, they would be receiving between $4,941 and $9,882. The largest of these payments are more than twice the size of current average EITC payments. Although the evaluations of the experiments are dated, they suggest that giving payments of this magnitude to low-income parents helped children in the poorest families.[38]

Frank O'Conner, Patrick Madden, and Allen Prindle studied the food intakes of rural children in North Carolina and Iowa. They found that in North Carolina the NIT children ate more, and ate better, than the children in households that did not receive payments—the NIT children increased their consumption of key nutrients including calcium, phosphorus, iron, riboflavin, and vitamin C. The Iowa NIT children, however, did not show any change in their food consumption. The researchers point out that the North Carolina children were poorer than the Iowa children, and so a possible explanation is that only the poorest children were at risk of nutritional deficiencies.

Rebecca Maynard and David Crawford examined the test scores of children in the same two sites, and found that in North Carolina, the NIT reduced absences, improved grades, and led to improved performance on achievement tests. In Iowa, however, there were no effects. Rebecca Maynard and Richard Murnane examined effects on the schooling of children in Gary, Indiana, another site where most of the families were extremely poor. They found that the NIT improved the reading scores of young children, and that the effects were largest for families that had been in the program for at least three years. Two studies, of children in New Jersey, and in Seattle and Denver, found that the NIT had large negative effects on the probability that teens dropped out of school.

Some of the most consistent effects of the NIT were on housing. A study of female-headed households in Seattle and Denver found that female-headed households were 50 percent more likely to buy a home if they were receiving NIT payments. Dale Poirier reports that African American households in New Jersey were also more likely to buy homes as a result of the NIT. Judith Wooldridge also found that renters in New Jersey increased their rental payments as a result of the NIT, while Marcy Avrin found that NIT families in the Seattle and Denver experiment were more likely to move out of public housing than other families. These improvements in housing are likely to have benefitted everyone in the family, including the children, as discussed further in chapter 4.

While these studies show that the NIT improved child outcomes and housing, researchers also found small effects on the purchase of "consumer durables," such as washing machines and cars. More recently, Lisa Barrow and Leslie McGranahan found that household spending on durables spikes in the month that families receive their EITC credit. One reason for this may be that households typically receive their EITC in one lump sum, even though it is possible to apply to have payments spread out through the year. The EITC offers families a way to save for "big ticket" items that they might not otherwise be able to afford.[39] Spending on these items may or may not benefit children, depending for instance, on whether or not they allow mothers to spend more time with their children.

Timothy Smeeding, Katherin Phillips, and Michael O'Connor recently conducted a study of EITC use among Chicago-area clients of a free tax preparation service. They find that while many families used the EITC simply to make ends meet (e.g., by paying off outstanding bills), others used it to invest in things that could improve their economic mobility, such as making tuition payments, upgrading their housing, or buying a car.[40] These findings indicate that families' receipt of payment in a lump sum may have important implications for the way that the money is spent, and for whether or not the spending benefits children.

It should not be surprising if it turns out that families do not spend all of the EITC on things that directly benefit children. Economic theory suggests that if parents value their own well-being as well as their children's, then any increase in income will pay for goods that benefit parents as well as children. Still, these studies show that large payments to families with children can improve outcomes in the poorest families. Under the EITC, the largest payments go to some of the poorest families, which suggests that the EITC provides a vital safety net for children in these families.

Alternative Income Support Mechanisms

If the main effect of the EITC is to give cash payments to poor working mothers, then it is worth asking whether the same goal could be met in a different way. Two alternatives that spring to mind are increases in the minimum wage, and child bonuses paid to mothers. Minimum wages are controversial, both inside and outside the Ivory Tower. The minimum wage used to be the "textbook" example of "The Law of Demand," which is the idea that when prices rise, purchases fall. When it is applied to the labor market, the law predicts that when minimum wages rise, some workers will lose their jobs.

In this scenario, there are winners and losers when minimum wages rise: winners take home fatter pay envelopes while losers become unemployed. At the household level, whether or not we care about such job losses depends in large part on which family members lose their jobs, and on where the family is in the income distribution. If the family bread winner becomes unemployed, this will cause a great deal more hardship than if a young middle-class teenager loses a source of pocket money.

The problem with this scenario is that the available evidence suggests that over the past twenty years, U.S. minimum wage increases have had little effect on low-wage employment. In their book *Myth and Measurement*, David Card and Alan Krueger criticize academics and policymakers for ignoring the accumulating evidence on this point.[41] While most economists have come around to the view that small increases in the minimum wage have at most small effects, few would feel sanguine about recommending really large increases.

One reason that economists are uncomfortable concluding that large minimum wage increases have little effect, is that the actual changes that have been studied did not occur randomly. Pressure to increase the minimum is likely to be higher in good times when wages are generally rising than in bad, and so a possible explanation for the muted effects that have been observed is that the hikes occurred at times when there was pent-up pressure for wages to rise.

A second problem with the minimum wage, at least from the perspective of assisting families with children, is that it is not explicitly targeted to these families. There is some debate about the extent to which minimum-wage workers are members of low-income families rather than, for example, teenagers from middle-class families. In 1988, California raised its minimum wage from $3.35 to $4.25 per hour. David Card's study of this increase suggested that half of teen workers were affected (i.e., had wages that were initially between $3.35 and $4.25) compared to only 11 percent of all California workers.[42] While many of these teens were from low-income families, 30 percent of minimum-wage workers were in families with incomes of $30,000 or more.

This study also highlights another potential downside of higher minimum wages: while employment among teenagers increased, schooling enrollments decreased, suggesting that teens were drawn out of school and into the work force by the higher minimum wage. Still, to the extent that the EITC increases labor supply and depresses wages, it would be sensible to regard the EITC and the minimum wage as complementary, rather than opposing, approaches to "making work pay"—it may be necessary to have a minimum-wage floor so that increases in the supply of low-wage labor that are caused by the EITC do not drive down wages.

The idea of a universal "baby bonus" payable to all families has an undeniable philosophical attraction. A universal payment would send the message that all children have value, and that the state has a direct responsibility to every child. In practice though, if the payment were treated as income for tax purposes, then low-income households would lose some of its value to taxes, while higher-income families would retain a large portion of the benefit even after taxes. Efforts to tinker with the credit so that more of it would be taxed back from high-income families would quickly lead us back to a credit administered through the tax system, with many of the same complexities as the EITC.[43]

Summary

In summary, single, unemployed mothers in 1990 were eligible for welfare benefits. In most states, the benefits left families well below the poverty line, scrambling to make up the difference through legal (but unreported) or illegal activities. Welfare reform was accompanied by a huge decrease in the welfare rolls, and an increase in the number of single, working mothers. But the evidence suggests that much of this change was accomplished through the carrots provided by plentiful jobs and the EITC supplement to earned income as well as through the sticks embodied in PRWORA. There is little evidence, though, that putting mothers to work has had much impact, positive or negative, on most poor children. Most newly employed mothers are not earning enough to raise them out of poverty without the earnings supplement provided by the EITC. The old welfare system has been replaced by one that rewards single mothers for working via the EITC, but still punishes them if they marry. Unlike welfare, EITC payments are large enough to have a significant impact on household incomes, and the available evidence suggests that these payments benefit children in the poorest households.

Chapter 2

In Sickness and in Health: The Importance of Public Health Insurance

Maria Torres had just lost Medicaid coverage for her two young sons. The program requires recipients to reapply for the program every six months. This time, Maria's monthly earnings had exceeded the state income cutoff for the program by $200. She immediately cut back on her hours as a domestic so that she would be able to qualify the next month. But four-year-old Roberto relies on medication to control his asthma and urgently needed to have his prescription renewed. Maria was shocked to find that Roberto's usual doctor would not see him because the family lacked insurance. She took time off work to take him to the Emergency Room, but the ER physician would not write a prescription: Roberto was not yet experiencing a medical emergency, and the doctor did not know the child. Finally, Maria phoned the original doctor's office in tears, explained the situation yet again, and was able to get the prescription phoned in to her local pharmacy.[1]

Maria and Roberto's story illustrates many features of the way that we provide medical care to vulnerable children. First and foremost, Roberto *is* generally eligible for public health insurance. This would not have been the case fifteen years ago, when a woman like Maria would have had to choose between holding a job or qualifying for public health insurance by going on welfare. This increase in coverage is a tremendous success story—but gaps in coverage, sometimes temporary, sometimes not, arise because of minor shifts in income or family circumstances as well as because of bureaucratic application procedures. These gaps mean that Roberto and myriad other children miss essential preventive services, such as the medication that he needs to keep his asthma under control.

Suppose that Roberto did not get his prescription, and had an acute asthma attack. If Roberto had arrived at the ER gasping for breath, he certainly would have been treated. The cost of the expensive emergency services would ultimately have been borne by the government, which subsidizes hospitals that provide indigent care, and by the privately insured, who are charged higher premiums. Thus, we all pay when children do not get the preventive care that they need and when the cost of emergency services is significantly higher than the cost of preventive treatment. One study found that the average emergency room visit for asthma cost $1,324 compared to $251 for outpatient treatment of asthma.[2]

This chapter details the public insurance safety net available to low-income women and children. The major change has been a dramatic expansion of eligibility for key programs over the past twenty years. Today about 40 percent of all births are paid for by government insurance. As of 2003, *all* poor children under nineteen are eligible for health insurance coverage under the Medicaid program. States have also extended eligibility for public health insurance under SCHIP (the State Child Health Insurance Program) to many children at higher income levels. In 2002, generous states, like Vermont and Connecticut, were covering children with family incomes up to $44,000.[3] These gains, however, are now threatened by Medicaid cutbacks in many states.

Problems of the Uninsured

The drive to extend public health insurance to uninsured women and children was grounded in research showing that lack of health insurance had serious consequences. Like Roberto, children without health insurance are significantly less likely to have a regular provider of care and five times more likely than other children to use an emergency room as a regular source of care. This lack of continuous care means that uninsured children are less likely to get important preventive services like checkups and vaccinations, and that critical problems may be overlooked or misdiagnosed. Uninsured children are less likely than other children to get medical attention when they are injured and are 25 percent more likely to miss school.[4]

The RAND Health Insurance experiment demonstrated that these effects really were due to the lack of insurance coverage, rather than to other factors like poverty or low maternal education, which are often associated with lack of coverage. This experiment, conducted from the mid-1970s to the early 1980s, randomly assigned approximately 2,000 families to either a free care "treatment group" or a control that had to pay some of the cost. All the plans were more generous than what was otherwise available to the families. Children eligible for free care were more likely to get preventive services (immunizations, vision examinations, and general medical exams) and more likely to get care for illnesses such as ear infections, acute upper respiratory infection, acute bronchitis, and common childhood injuries.[5]

This research strongly suggested that increasing health insurance for poor women and children would improve their health, and that it might also reduce health-care costs. Policymakers responded with dramatic increases in eligibility for coverage. The expansion's effects on insurance coverage, utilization of care, and health clearly show that expanding eligibility for insurance had positive effects.

Yet the uninsured remain a staple of newspaper headlines. As the *Washington Post* put it in 2003, "Shawn Hegdal of Bozeman, Mont., has no health insurance. But that's old news. Shawn Hegdal still has no health insurance. That's today's headline." The fraction of children without health insurance has hovered near 12 percent for the past decade despite the expansions in eligibility for pubic health insurance. Even as eligibility for public health insurance has expanded, many children have lost private health insurance coverage as the cost of these policies has continued to rise. Other uninsured children are eligible for public health insurance but do not take it up. And hard-won gains in children's insurance coverage are threatened by state budget cutbacks that have reduced the amount of money available for these programs.[6]

Expansions of Public Insurance under the Medicaid Program and SCHIP

Medicaid is a public health insurance program that covers poor women and children, along with those who are disabled, and some elderly. Slightly less than half of Medicaid recipients are children, while another fifth are low-income women. Yet, although they account for three quarters of the recipients, women and children account for only about a quarter of Medicaid expenditures. The lion's share of the spending is on the elderly and disabled. For example, in 2000 the government spent $1,237 per child on Medicaid compared to $11,928 per elderly adult. By 2003, the projected cost of Medicaid had grown to $280 billion dollars, which means that even the fraction of those dollars devoted to women and children (about $44.6 billion) dwarfed the approximately $16 billion per year spent on traditional cash welfare under the TANF program. We can also compare spending for mothers and children to the huge expenditures made under the Medi*care* program. Medicare, the main public health insurance program for people over sixty-five, cost $239 billion in 2003.[7]

The costs of Medicaid are shared by states and the federal government. To receive their federal "match," states are required to run the programs within certain guidelines, which used to require that families be on welfare. The linkage of Medicaid with AFDC restricted access to the program in three ways. First, since cash welfare was normally available only to single mothers, Medicaid was not an option for most two-parent families. Second, income cutoffs for cash welfare varied across states and were often very low. For example, the income cutoff in South Carolina in 1984 was only 29 percent of the federal poverty line—in 2004, this would have meant an income cutoff of only $4,500 for a family of three! Third, the stigma and other problems associated with applying for cash welfare programs may have kept some eligible families from applying for either welfare or Medicaid benefits.[8]

Congress began to break the link between Medicaid and AFDC with the Deficit Reduction Act of 1984.[9] This legislation required states to cover all children in families whose incomes made them eligible for AFDC, as long as the children were born after September 1, 1983. In other words, families with children less than one year old were initially covered under the new legislation. Families with older children were to be phased in one year at a time in succeeding years. This legislation allowed two-parent families to apply, though this was largely a symbolic measure since few two-parent families were poor enough to be eligible.

The 1984 legislation was followed by a series of measures that raised the income cutoffs for children's Medicaid eligibility above the old welfare cutoffs. By July 1, 1991, states were required to cover all children under age nineteen whose family incomes were below the poverty line (as long as those children were born after September 30, 1983). By 2003 all poor children were eligible for Medicaid, a remarkable legislative accomplishment.

The law changes typically first gave states the option of receiving federal matching funds to cover a particular group (such as children under five with incomes less than the federal poverty line), and then required states to cover the group in order to continue to receive any federal Medicaid funds. The 1997 budget agreement continued this pattern by setting aside an additional $24 billion to fund state health insurance programs aimed at extending health insurance for children. This initiative became known as the State Child Health Insurance Program (or SCHIP), and by April 1998, about 1.2 million children had gained eligibility for health insurance coverage under the program.[10]

Legislators also targeted pregnant women. Beginning in the early 1980s, Medicaid benefits became available to pregnant women with incomes below welfare cutoffs who had been ineligible because they did not already have a child, to pregnant teens in families with incomes less than the welfare cutoff regardless of family structure, and to women in two-parent families with incomes less than the welfare income cutoffs. In April 1987, income cutoffs for pregnant women were greatly liberalized. By April 1990, a uniform minimum threshold had been established—the new guidelines required that all states wishing to participate in the Medicaid program cover pregnant women (and children under six) with incomes up to 133 percent of the poverty line, and states had the option of receiving matching funds to cover women with incomes up to 185 percent of the poverty line. These new guidelines meant that for the first time, women in families with incomes up to $29,000 (using the poverty cutoff for a family of 3 in 2004) were eligible for benefits. And for the first time, the Medicaid safety net would be uniform across the country, rather than being less generous in poorer states.

Through this combination of carrots and sticks, states were all gradually brought up to the same, more generous, standard. Given that they started at different levels and took up the expansion options at different rates, income thresholds for Medicaid eligibility, however, varied wildly across states in the intervening years. For example, in Texas, only 3 percent of pregnant women would have been eligible for Medicaid coverage in 1979, while half were eligible by 1992. By contrast, in more generous states like New York, a quarter of women were eligible in 1979, while, again, half were eligible by 1992.

Many state governments went beyond the federal Medicaid expansions and used their own funds to extend Medicaid coverage to otherwise ineligible women and children. In October 1997 (a year after TANF began to be implemented), forty-one states were using their own funds to extend Medicaid coverage to women and children in families with incomes up to two or three times the federal poverty level.[11]

Several states also developed their own programs to cover children who were ineligible for Medicaid. MinnesotaCare, initiated in 1992, covered children between the ages of one and eighteen who live in families with incomes at or below 275 percent of the federal poverty level ($44,138 for a family of four in 1997), provided those children were state residents and did not have access to employer-sponsored health care. MinnesotaCare was funded by a tax on health-care providers and by enrollment premiums set on a sliding scale. Pennsylvania, Vermont, and Washington adopted similar, publicly funded programs.

A second state model for providing health insurance to children involved public and private partnerships. The Florida Healthy Kids program, which started in 1990, was initially funded by the private Robert Wood Johnson Foundation. By 1995 the budget drew on federal Medicaid funds, general state revenues, local government funds, and family contributions. The program negotiated with private health maintenance organizations to provide coverage for the children and subsidized the premiums of low-income children on a sliding scale. New York, Colorado, and New Hampshire adopted similar programs.

Many of these stand-alone efforts were incorporated into the new SCHIP program, which allowed states to choose whether to insure more children either by expanding Medicaid or by developing similar stand-alone programs. The rapid expansion of public health insurance under the Medicaid program and SCHIP offered a unique opportunity to measure the effects of health insurance on child health because many people became eligible without any other change in their circumstances. Evaluations of the effects of the expansions leave little doubt that they improved the health of poor children. Even in crude indicators of health status like mortality, the effects of the Medicaid expansions are readily apparent.

Measuring the Effects of the Expansions

Measurement of the effects of the expansions is complicated by the fact that poorer states are likely to have both poorer child outcomes and a higher fraction of their population who are eligible for Medicaid. For example, it would not be surprising to find that infant mortality was higher in Mississippi than in New York, in part because there are more poor people (as a fraction of the population) in Mississippi. Yet because there are more poor people in Mississippi, any given increase in Medicaid eligibility is likely to make more people eligible there than in New York. This means that comparing the means across states is likely to understate the true effect of the Medicaid expansions because places where the expansions had more impact on coverage would also have had poorer infant outcomes in any case.

In a series of studies, Jonathan Gruber and I proposed a method for isolating the effects of Medicaid rules by constructing an index of the generosity of the rules in each state. Variation in this index comes only from differences in the state Medicaid rules, and not from differences in poverty rates or other economic or demographic characteristics of the states. Using this index, we found that the 30 percent increase in the eligibility of pregnant women that took place during the 1980s and early 1990s was associated with an 8.5 percent decline in the infant mortality rate. This decline corresponds to 2,400 lives saved per year. The roughly 15 percent increase in Medicaid eligibility for children that occurred over the same period reduced child mortality by 8 percent. This decline occurred only for deaths from internal causes, with no decline in deaths from external causes such as accidents, which supports the conclusion that the decline in deaths reflects the effects of the Medicaid expansions—deaths from internal causes should be more sensitive to insurance-induced improvements in personal medical care than are deaths from external causes like accidents.[12]

We also examined the effects on utilization of care directly, and found that becoming eligible for Medicaid reduced the probability that a child went without any doctor visits during the year by 9.6 percentage points. Roughly 20 percent of children receive no doctor visits at all in a given year—although it is recommended that children receive at least an annual checkup. Our results suggest that this number would have been closer to 30 percent in the absence of the Medicaid expansions, so that as many as six million children gained a doctor's visit.

It is less expensive to treat many illnesses in a doctor's office than in a hospital emergency room or clinic, and so we also looked at the site of care for children who had had a doctor visit in the past two weeks. We found a significant increase in the fraction of those visits that took place in doctors' offices. This is consistent with data from case studies in states like Florida, which found that extensions of insurance coverage to uninsured children reduced emergency room visits by 70 percent, saving the state $13 million in 1996.[13]

Several studies have examined the effects of the Medicaid and SCHIP expansions on hospitalizations among children. There are many conditions, like asthma, that should never lead to hospitalization if they are properly managed. Hence, the hospitalization of a child who has been diagnosed with asthma represents a failure of preventive care. Anna Aizer studied a California outreach program that offered community organizations $50 for their assistance with each successful application for public health insurance. This program not only increased enrollment but also reduced hospitalizations for preventable illnesses.[14] Leemore Dafny and Jonathan Gruber find that nationally, expansions in Medicaid eligibility led to a 22 percent decline in preventable hospitalizations.[15]

Judged by the most obvious criteria, the Medicaid expansions were a great success. They were intended to improve infant and child health, and they did. They reduced mortality, decreased the number of children going without care, increased access to doctors' offices, and reduced ER visits and preventable hospitalizations. A closer look, though, reveals limits on what extensions of eligibility for health insurance can accomplish.

Despite the great success of the Medicaid expansions and of SCHIP, many people eligible for public health insurance do not sign up. As a result, they do not receive the preventive services that they need. In the case of pregnant women, the consequences are easy to see: The Medicaid expansions reduced infant mortality but had little overall effect on the incidence of low birth weight (birth weight less than 2,500 grams). Low birth weight is the key indicator of the health of an infant at birth. If infants were no healthier at birth, but were still more likely to live, then this suggests that the gains were the result of high-tech interventions that took place at the time of the birth and afterward, rather than the consequence of improvement in underlying fetal health brought about, for example, by improvements in prenatal care.

Technological miracles are performed in neonatal intensive care units across the country every day, but these miracles have a high cost both in terms of dollars and in the human toll. The struggle to save one "preemie" was documented in *U.S. News and World Reports*. Born after only twenty-five weeks gestation, the baby weighed only 12.5 ounces, 135 grams less than what was thought to be the minimum weight necessary for survival. She spent 133 days in a neonatal intensive care unit at $1,500 per day for a total cost of $199,500. This baby escaped damage to her major organs, but it was not clear at the time of her release from the hospital whether she would be able to see normally. Moreover, recent research has shown that surviving infants with very low birth weights are at high risk of conditions such as cerebral palsy and mental retardation. While it is not clear whether this particular baby's problems could have been prevented, every premature birth that can be prevented through improved prenatal care reduces trauma, future disabilities, and public expense.[16]

Initially utilization of prenatal care was not improved by the Medicaid expansions, because many newly eligible women were not aware that they were eligible for Medicaid. Newly eligible women could be divided into two groups: very low-income women who were familiar with the welfare system and with the Medicaid program, and higher-income women who had never before been eligible for any form of public assistance. When Jon Gruber and I made this distinction, we found that the fraction of newly eligible women who actually became covered was much higher among the poorest women than among women with somewhat higher incomes.

Not surprisingly then, although the expansions had no effect on the overall incidence of low birth weight, they did have an effect among the poorest. This improvement in birth weight in the poorest group was linked to reduced delays in initiating prenatal care. We estimate that in this group, becoming eligible for Medicaid reduced by half the probability that care was delayed beyond the first trimester.

The data on Medicaid expenditures are consistent with this broad picture—expansions of eligibility to the poorer group increased Medicaid expenditures on both outpatient care (which includes most prenatal visits) and inpatient care. Expansions of eligibility to women of slightly higher income only increased inpatient hospital costs. The evidence all suggests that women familiar with public assistance programs were more likely to learn that they were eligible for Medicaid in time to use it to get prenatal care. In contrast, women of slightly higher income did not know that they were eligible, and may have learned of their eligibility only when they arrived at the hospital to deliver.

The evidence is also mixed with respect to the utilization of care among children. While the Dafny and Gruber study showed large declines in preventable hospitalizations, there were increases in hospitalizations for other conditions, so that in total, the Medicaid expansions led to a 10 percent increase in pediatric hospitalizations. There was also a shifting of patients from public to private hospitals. It is difficult to know without more information whether the increase in hospitalizations at private hospitals represented an increase in access to necessary, high-quality care for sick children, or an increase in unnecessary hospitalizations that was motivated by the higher ability to pay among parents/guardians of the newly-covered children.

Problems with Take-up of Public Insurance

Unlike their patients, hospital administrators are generally well informed about Medicaid rules. Hospitals have strong incentives to make sure that Medicaid-eligible pregnant women register at the time of their admission, because they are forbidden to turn away women in labor, and are thus forced to provide uncompensated care to uninsured low-income mothers who do not sign up for Medicaid. In fact, before the Medicaid expansions, childbirth was the single largest component of uncompensated charges to hospitals. The incentive to assist otherwise uninsured women to sign up for Medicaid has always been present, but it became much stronger with the Medicaid expansions, since more of the uninsured became eligible, thereby offering greater savings to more hospitals. The U.S. General Accounting Office reported that many hospitals established Medicaid offices on site, or contracted with private firms to help Medicaid-eligible patients navigate the often tortuous route to claiming benefits.[17]

As of the early 1990s, many eligible women were enrolled in Medicaid at the point of delivery, too late to receive the prenatal care that would have improved the health of their unborn children. This pattern of resource utilization is inhumane. Even if they do not die, unhealthy infants are at risk for developmental problems in later life. It is also extremely inefficient. We estimated that it cost $840,000 (in 1986 dollars) to save an infant life through the expansions of eligibility to the poorest women. In contrast, it cost $4.2 million to save a life by expanding eligibility for Medicaid to women of higher-income levels. The reason is that the poor women took advantage of the program to receive better prenatal care. Richer women may not have even learned that they were eligible until they arrived at the hospital to deliver. Hence, the infants of richer women were saved through the application of expensive high-tech neonatal care rather than through less expensive preventive prenatal care.

Over the past decade, states have made a great effort to get Medicaid-eligible pregnant women into prenatal care. Nevada implemented a program called "Baby Your Baby," which consists of an aggressive advertising campaign for prenatal care, along with a toll-free number that people can call for information about providers of prenatal care in their area. Infant mortality in the state declined from nine deaths per 1,000 before implementation of the program to 5.7 deaths per 1,000. The percentage of pregnant women receiving prenatal care in the first trimester climbed from 68 to 79 percent during the campaign, and 83 percent of women delivering in Nevada have heard of the program and know that it offers access to prenatal services. This program cost only $468,000 in fiscal year 1997. California adopted a similar program, with the result that the fraction of women beginning prenatal care in the first trimester increased from 72 to 84 percent over the 1990s.[18]

On the other hand, the fraction of children without health insurance has been remarkably constant in the face of the expansions. Only 62 percent of poor children are covered. Despite the existence of Medicaid and SCHIP, 8.5 million children (or 11.6 percent of all children) had no health insurance in 2002. Nine out of ten of these children have parents who work, and 60 percent of them live in two-parent families. These figures suggest that lack of "take-up" among low-income children remains a significant problem. David Card and Lara Shore-Sheppard find that expansions of eligibility to all poor children born after September 30, 1983, led to only about a 10 percentage point rise in Medicaid coverage for children born just after the cutoff date, while further expansions of Medicaid eligibility to children under six in families with incomes below 133 percent of the poverty line had even smaller effects.[19]

Why don't parents of children eligible for free health insurance sign them up? As Roberto's story illustrates, the simplest explanation is that it is time-consuming and difficult to maintain a child's enrollment in Medicaid, and in an emergency, health services paid for by the Medicaid program will be available in any case. Applicants for Medicaid are usually required to show birth certificates or citizenship papers, rent receipts, or utility bills to prove residency, and pay stubs as proof of income. Until recently, applicants were required to document the value of cars and assets such as insurance policies. Many states have a time limit on the number of days the applicant can take to provide documentation, and applicants must attend interviews with case workers, who review the entire application package and make the final determination of eligibility. Between one-third and one-half of all Medicaid applications are denied, often for procedural reasons—applicants are not able to document their eligibility or do not show up for all the required interviews.

Welfare case workers are generally required to provide basic assistance to applicants in completing application forms—but they may not be able to provide the intensive help some applicants need to get through the process. Also, as a consequence of expansions in

Medicaid and contractions in cash welfare, many eligible women and families are not on welfare and have no access to these case workers. Federal fraud prevention efforts create a disincentive for states to provide application assistance. States are penalized (through reductions in federal Medicaid matching funds) if they provide benefits to too many people who aren't actually eligible. Yet there is no penalty for turning away people who are eligible. This system encourages states to "play it safe" and err on the side of denying benefits to qualified applicants.[20]

Families who successfully negotiate the system once must periodically requalify for Medicaid, sometimes every six months. This need to verify Medicaid eligibility may account for some of the "churning" in the Medicaid caseload. One study found that only 43 percent of Medicaid patients stayed on the program continuously for a thirty-two-month period, and that over half of those leaving the program remained uninsured. These gaps in coverage mean that parents may delay obtaining preventive care for their children.

Medicaid enrollments for children follow a seasonal pattern. They are higher in summer and fall than in winter or spring, which suggests that some parents may go through the Medicaid enrollment process annually to get preventive care that is necessary for school enrollment, such as immunizations. They then allow the coverage to lapse until the next time that there is an urgent need for it. One study of 500 Latino children found that 69 percent had received only one doctor's visit in the past year and that in 20 percent of these cases the visit was for school-related purposes.[21]

Families may also be reluctant to go through the onerous enrollment process because in a real medical emergency care is available to everyone regardless of insurance status. Thus, many eligibles may decide that the benefits of enrolling are just not worth the costs of applying. The system creates a strong incentive for families to forgo preventive care (which they must pay for out of pocket if they are uninsured) and to use medical care only in case of emergency. They may also try to use emergency rooms for routine medical care.

Hospitals reinforce these incentives. Hospitals must provide emergency care regardless of the patient's ability to pay, and so if the patient cannot pay, the hospital ends up absorbing the cost of the "uncompensated care." When an emergency patient without insurance arrives, the hospital has several options. First, it can illegally "dump" the patient by turning him or her away. In this case, the hospital may incur a financial liability if the patient dies or suffers injury because the hospital refused to provide care. Secondly, the hospital can provide care and then attempt to get reimbursed by the patient. For example, it could try to garnish the future wages of uninsured patients. A problem with this option is that it is difficult to wring blood from stones: Uninsured patients who face steep medical bills may never be able to pay. This is why medical expenses have become one of the leading causes of bankruptcy filings.[22]

The third option is for the hospital to assist eligible uninsured people to enroll in Medicaid. This is likely to be a much more cost-effective option than attempting to obtain reimbursement from low-income individuals. As a result, many hospitals have established Medicaid enrollment offices on site, which assist people in completing applications and tell them how to obtain necessary documentation.

Hospitals in most states also employ private firms to help them enroll eligible patients in the Medicaid program. These firms offer a wide range of assistance that understaffed welfare offices are often unable to provide. For example, if they get power-of-attorney from patients, they can then track down documents such as birth certificates, bank statements, and rent receipts. Helping people enroll in the Medicaid program can be a lucrative business. In fiscal year 1992, one hospital paid an enrollment vendor firm $2 million in return for enrollment efforts that resulted in an additional $10 million in revenues from Medicaid.[23]

As a General Accounting Office report makes clear, the efforts made by these firms can be quite aggressive:

> The child of a single, uninsured, working mother incurred a $20,000 hospital bill. . . . The hospital referred this case to an enrollment vendor firm after determining that it was a potential Medicaid case. After contacting the mother, the firm initiated

and submitted a Medicaid application. The firm gave the applicant a list of verification items she would have to provide. However, the applicant did not provide the requested items and Medicaid coverage was denied. Upon learning of the denial, the firm contacted the applicant twice weekly for a period of 2 months to get her to cooperate. . . . Eventually, the applicant responded and submitted the verification items and a signed power of attorney to the firm. . . . The signed power of attorney allowed the firm to appeal the denial successfully.[24]

This mother had little incentive to cooperate with the hospital since the care that the child needed had already been provided. Only the repeated harassment of the agency resulted in Medicaid coverage of the child, which could be applied retroactively to cover the hospital's expenses. It seems unlikely that this child's Medicaid coverage was renewed the next time it lapsed. The mother may not have valued the free preventive care offered by Medicaid, and the hospital had already demonstrated that it would provide free care in an emergency.

Given the incentives that are built into the system, it is not surprising that expanding eligibility for public insurance does not always result in the most efficient pattern of utilization of medical resources. The incentives point toward letting coverage lapse until a medical crisis brings hospital agencies in to assist parents in enrolling their children. The spotty take-up of Medicaid coverage by eligible children suggests that Medicaid is far more important than coverage numbers would suggest. Even children who are not enrolled often count on and receive assistance paid for by the Medicaid program in the event of a medical emergency. So at any point in time, many more children rely on Medicaid than are captured by official statistics.

The early experiences of families subject to welfare reform provide some additional evidence about the difficulty of translating eligibility into coverage. In principle, the replacement of AFDC by TANF with its time-limited welfare benefits should have had little effect on child Medicaid caseloads. Among children, eligibility for

Medicaid no longer had much to do with being on welfare: The Medicaid expansions had broken the tight link between being on welfare and eligibility for Medicaid. Families that left welfare were unlikely to leave it for well-paid jobs with health insurance coverage, and so they still needed the Medicaid program. Yet census estimates suggested that as many as 1 million children lost Medicaid benefits as a result of their parents leaving the welfare rolls. When Wisconsin implemented aggressive programs to get people off cash welfare, Medicaid enrollments dropped by 40 to 50 percent among those who were forced off.[25]

The reason these children lost their benefits is that it is much easier for children of welfare mothers to enroll in Medicaid. People on welfare are automatically eligible for Medicaid, and so welfare mothers do not have to go through any additional application process. In contrast, mothers who left the welfare rolls did have to deal with the application process if they wanted their children to remain insured. The dramatic fall in Medicaid caseloads with welfare reform shows that many former welfare mothers had a great deal of difficulty dealing with this application process.

The California study by Anna Aizer discussed earlier indicates that community-based outreach can be effective. Another study examining differences in SCHIP programs across states finds that while take-up is generally low, measures such as eliminating asset tests, offering continuous coverage, and simplifying the application process increase take-up rates. Mandatory waiting periods, however, which have been introduced or extended in many states because of budget crises, consistently reduce take-up.[26]

The Quality of Public Health Insurance

Gaining public insurance coverage will not help children if doctors do not accept it. Twenty percent of U.S. pediatricians refuse to see Medicaid patients at all, and 40 percent limit the number of Medicaid patients in their practices. Moreover, both percentages have been growing over time as more and more physicians opt out of the Medicaid program. In 1977, only 15 percent of physicians refused Medicaid patients and only 26 percent limited their numbers.[27]

The result is that while children on Medicaid are more likely than uninsured children to have a usual source of care, and to receive routine care on an appropriate schedule, they are less likely to be seen in doctor's offices. Instead they may receive routine care at a clinic, and sick care in a hospital emergency room, which means that they lack continuity of care. Children on Medicaid are less likely to see specialists than other children—54 percent see a general practitioner compared to 34 percent of non-Medicaid children. Also, children on Medicaid have doctor visits that are up to 40 percent shorter (relative to the average visit time of thirteen minutes) than non-Medicaid children.[28]

These differences in care can have real consequences. For example, a 1995 New York State Health Department study found that death rates among infants of healthy birth weight were 30 percent higher in public hospitals (which have higher Medicaid caseloads) than in private hospitals. One public hospital in Brooklyn had nearly twice the rate of deaths among babies of normal birth weight as the private hospital across the street. As Congressman Henry Waxman has remarked, "[M]erely having a Medicaid card does not, in and of itself, assure access to physician services."[29]

Doctors give many reasons for limiting participation in the Medicaid program, but one of the most frequently cited is simple frustration with Medicaid bureaucracy. Doctors complain that there is more red tape under Medicaid than under private insurance; that Medicaid often uses a different claim form from other insurers and different procedure or diagnosis codes, requiring a separate computer system; and that claims are paid late, or are frequently denied on a technicality. Some states have different rules and reimbursement schedules for clinics, hospitals, and private physician offices, so that doctors who practice in more than one setting must negotiate several sets of procedures. States been known to run out of funds mid-year and to deny any further claims until they get more money at the beginning of the next fiscal year. Physicians also complain that states often change the rules without notifying them until claims are denied. These problems have lead many physicians to conclude that it is not worth their while to serve Medicaid patients.[30]

One study of obstetrician/gynecologists found that doctors were significantly more likely to participate in the Medicaid program in states in which an outside agent did the Medicaid claims processing instead of a state agency. Presumably, these doctors experienced fewer difficulties in having claims reimbursed than those facing state agencies. Doctors in states that impose limits on the services that are covered or that require physicians to obtain prior authorization for certain services were less likely to participate in the program.[31]

Fear of legal liability is a second often-cited concern of physicians who avoid Medicaid patients. One way to reduce exposure to lawsuits is to try to screen out patients who are high risk. Doctors know that Medicaid patients are poorer and likely to be less educated than the privately insured. On average, Medicaid patients are also more likely to receive inadequate prenatal care (though ironically this may be in part because doctors refuse to see them), and to have problems such as drug or alcohol dependence that put their babies at risk. Doctors see Medicaid patients as more likely to have serious medical problems, more likely to miss appointments, and less compliant than other patients. Therefore, a doctor who wants to avoid high-risk patients, or limit the number of such patients, may turn away Medicaid patients. Medicaid coverage can be identified over the phone, before the potential patient has even made an appointment. So it is natural for doctors to use it as an indicator, albeit an imperfect one, for risk status.[32]

Carol Korenbrot's survey of obstetrician/gynecologists in New York state found that about half of those currently treating Medicaid patients and a fifth of those excluding Medicaid patients said that they would expand the number of Medicaid patients in their practices in response to liability reform. The doctors viewed three possible reforms—ceilings on litigation awards, no-fault insurance, and a subsidy for liability expenses—equally favorably. What doctors say that they would do in a hypothetical situation and what they would actually do are not necessarily the same. The survey does highlight, however, many doctors' belief that liability issues are a significant deterrent to treating Medicaid patients.[33]

Red tape and fear of lawsuits notwithstanding, the most important obstacle to providing care for more Medicaid patients in the view of many physicians is low reimbursements by the Medicaid program. Comparisons of Medicaid payments to those made under Medicare (which pays for the health care of the elderly) indicate that Medicaid pays only about 66 percent as much. For pediatric or obstetric services, which are not covered by Medicare, Medicaid pays about half as much as do private insurers. If Medicaid patients are more of a hassle (or perceived as such), higher risk, and pay half as much as other patients, it is no wonder that many doctors have decided not to treat them.[34]

An unusual unanimity marks the findings of the many studies that have examined the effects of fees on doctor participation in the Medicaid program. They all find that higher fees encourage doctors to participate, accept more Medicaid patients, and see more of them in private offices rather than public settings. Higher fees may influence not only whether people are treated but also how they are treated. A California project paid obstetricians/gynecologists an extra $50 per patient if the patient began prenatal care within the first trimester, $111 if the patient completed four risk assessments (for clinical, psycho-social, nutrition, and health education) in the first month of care, and $100 if the patient completed ten or more prenatal visits. Women who received care from providers in this program had significantly fewer low birth weight babies than those who received care from regular Medicaid providers, suggesting that they received better care.[35]

Similarly, Sandra Decker finds that doctors in states with higher Medicaid reimbursements spent more time per visit with their Medicaid patients. In work with Jon Gruber and Michael Fischer, I have found that states with higher Medicaid reimbursement rates tend to have lower infant mortality rates, which reflects both a higher probability of pregnant women and infants receiving care, as well as higher quality service. Conversely, low Medicaid reimbursement rates push patients out of doctors' offices and into hospital emergency rooms and outpatient clinics.[36]

Low reimbursements are a problem for hospitals as well as for office-based physicians. In testimony before the Senate Finance Committee, Dr. George Farr, President of the Children's Medical Center of Dallas, noted that on average hospitals are reimbursed only 75 cents for every dollar that they spend on children. In many instances, they are reimbursed much less. He offered the example of Maria, a three-year-old Medicaid patient admitted for congestive heart failure who required more than four months of care at a cost of $234,000 (in 1989 dollars). The hospital was reimbursed only $50,000 because this was the cap on reimbursements for hospital care in Texas. Dr. Farr remarked that given dollar limits on coverage and length-of-stay, higher survival rates for children meant that his hospital incurred more financial liability.[37]

While children shouldn't have to miss out on the care they need, it is also possible that otherwise uninsured women and children who become eligible for Medicaid will receive unnecessary care, which inflates costs. Jonathan Gruber and I have shown that new mothers who were likely to be eligible for Medicaid because of their demographic characteristics and state of residence were more likely to have had a range of obstetrical procedures, including fetal monitoring, ultrasounds, induction of labor, and Caesarian sections. A Caesarian is both more convenient for doctors and more profitable than a regular delivery, and doctors can bill more for procedures such as fetal monitoring and ultrasounds, whether or not these procedures improve health outcomes.[38]

In the United States, between 8 and 35 percent of babies are delivered by Caesarean depending on the part of the country. This geographical variation is related to medical capacity rather than to medical need. While there is no doubt that some lives are saved by Caesarians, the United States has a much higher rate than countries like Great Britain, which have lower infant mortality rates; and the rate of Caesarian sections climbed rapidly in the United States in the 1980s. These facts suggest that increases in the utilization of Cesarians are not necessarily linked to infant health.[39]

In my work with Jon Gruber, we found no evidence that the additional utilization of procedures like Cesarians that was induced by the Medicaid expansions saved lives, although it no doubt added to the high costs per life saved. These results are consistent with those of Jennifer Hass and her collaborators who found in a Massachusetts case study that the Medicaid expansions led to an increase in the rate of Caesarian section delivery without any change in infant health outcomes.[40]

Increases in the amount of unnecessary care may be a side effect of providing insurance, but the problem is certainly not unique to Medicaid. There is a large literature on what is called "induced demand," or the idea that doctors can increase the demand for their services unnecessarily. The main problem is that doctors typically have much better information than patients about the type of care that is needed. If the doctor insists that a Caesarian is necessary, few parents are going to argue, because the risk associated with undergoing an unnecessary procedure is small, while the risk associated with ignoring the doctor's advice is very great.

David Cutler, who served on the Clinton administration's health care reform task force, has proposed that this problem could be solved by paying doctors on the basis of the quality rather than the quantity of care provided. If Roberto is hospitalized for asthma, then the hospital will be reimbursed—but the hospital is not reimbursed for time spent helping Maria to gain access to the medications necessary to prevent the hospitalization. In fact, Roberto's main problem is that he is allergic to mold, which is growing under the leaky kitchen sink in his home. Maria has complained to her landlord about the leak several times, but the landlord refuses to fix it. The real cure for Roberto's asthma would be to force the landlord to comply with existing codes, fix the leak, and remove the mold. If the hospital were reimbursed for providing a public health nurse who could establish contact with Maria, monitor Roberto's medications, and put her in touch with a housing rights advocacy group, then Roberto's health would be greatly improved. We need a system that provides incentives for the medical establishment to provide the most effective care, rather than the costliest care.[41]

Public Insurance and the "Crowd-out" of Private Insurance

It should not surprise us that some children eligible for Medicaid did not take up their benefits. Only two-thirds of those eligible for cash welfare or food stamps use these programs, perhaps because those who are only eligible for a short time do not find it worthwhile to go through the administrative procedures necessary to sign up. Nevertheless, a Medicaid take-up rate of less than 25 percent among newly eligible children seems unusually low. Jonathan Gruber and David Cutler have argued that one reason for the low take-up is that as many as two-thirds of the children made eligible for Medicaid already had private health insurance coverage. If all of the children who came onto the rolls would otherwise have been uninsured, then the take-up rate among these uninsured children would have been closer to 70 percent, a figure in line with the take-up rates for cash welfare and food stamps.[42]

It is possible that some of the children who came onto the roles would have had private insurance in the absence of the Medicaid expansions, and so this figure is an upper bound on true take-up rates. In fact, the Medicaid expansions may have had the perverse effect of actually causing a decline in private health insurance coverage. Ideally, new enrollees in Medicaid or SCHIP would come only from the uninsured population. Increases in the fraction of children covered by public insurance would then result in dramatic increases in the fraction of children with health insurance coverage. The raw numbers show that this did not happen—decreases in private health insurance coverage for children roughly kept pace with the increases in Medicaid coverage so that there was little net increase in the fraction of children insured.

Families might drop their private health insurance to take advantage of the free care provided under Medicaid. Or employers might decide not to offer health insurance if many of their employees were eligible for public health insurance. To take an extreme case, suppose that all of the new Medicaid enrollees would have been covered by private insurance in the absence of the expansions. Then the expansions would have resulted in a considerable increase in public expenditures with no improvement in the fraction of children insured. It is possible that families of children who "switched" from the private to the public program were made better off—most private insurance plans have co-payments and many do not cover pediatric preventive services at all, while under Medicaid most services are completely free. Still, a replacement of private with public insurance is not what Congress had in mind when it mandated expanded insurance coverage.

Medicaid expansions could not have been responsible for all of the decline in private health insurance coverage among women and children, because private insurance coverage rates for groups that one would not expect to have been affected by the expansions (such as young single men) are also falling. In fact, private health insurance coverage has been declining for all groups, although it has been falling twice as quickly for children as for adults.[43]

One might conclude then, that about half of the decline in private health insurance coverage among children could be attributed to children moving from private to public insurance in response to the Medicaid expansions. This is in fact the conclusion of one of the most careful studies of the causal effect of the expansions on private health insurance coverage. David Cutler and Jon Gruber conclude that 3.5 million people gained public coverage and 1.7 million lost private health insurance coverage as a direct result of the Medicaid expansions.[44]

This estimate has proven extremely controversial because it implies that some of the money that government spent to cover uninsured children was wasted in the sense that it just replaced private health insurance coverage with public coverage. Other researchers pose the "crowd-out question" in somewhat different ways, and come up with smaller numbers. For example, Lisa Dubay and Genevieve Kenney point out that much of the increase in Medicaid coverage over the period occurred among people who would have been eligible even in the absence of the Medicaid expansions, so that these people cannot be said to have been "crowded out" of private health insurance by the Medicaid expansions. They estimate that only 15 percent of the decline in overall private insurance coverage over the 1987–92 period resulted from the Medicaid expansions, which suggests that we need more information about the underlying causes of the continuing erosion of the private health insurance system. The most likely cause is the continuing increase in the costs of medical care and hence in the cost of insurance, though good systematic data on the costs of private insurance plans are hard to find.[45]

Public Health Insurance and Managed Care

Much of what we know about the effects of insurance coverage, or the lack of it, comes from studies of traditional fee-for-service health insurance programs. In fee-for-service plans, people can choose any physician, and the physician can bill the insurance company (or Medicaid) for any services rendered—but both the publicly insured and the privately insured are increasingly being enrolled in some form of "managed care," with restrictions both on whom they can see and what services are covered. By 2000, 54 percent of the children in Medicaid were covered by managed care.[46]

Some features of managed care, such as coordination of care by case managers and the designation of clearly identifiable providers, have the potential greatly to improve access to care. For example, a case manager could help a family find both a general practitioner and a specialist who accepted Medicaid payments—but the evidence to date is mixed. A 1995 review of over 130 studies of Medicaid managed care by the Kaiser Foundation found that the switch to managed care reduced the utilization of emergency room and specialist care but did not lead to any consistent changes in the overall number of doctor visits. Similarly, access to preventive care did not seem to rise or fall consistently, and it remained lower for the Medicaid population than for the non-poor population.[47]

Several General Accounting Office reports have criticized quality control standards in Medicaid managed care plans. For example, a 1995 study found that California had no way of verifying whether children in these programs had actually received necessary preventive services. For instance, providers were required to submit information about the fraction of children in their practices with up-to-date immunizations but were not required to show that any individual child had been immunized.[48]

Problems with quality control may be particularly acute in the Medicaid population because of administrative "churning": Many people are not continually covered but repeatedly enter and exit the program, making it difficult to keep track of their health-care needs. For example, in many systems, patients receive a new case number every time they enter the system. Many Medicaid managed care plans give clients very little choice about who their provider will be—the provider agrees to accept a low fixed payment per patient from the state with the understanding that the patient will stay with that provider. Since there is little monitoring of the services that are actually provided, and since patients cannot "vote with the feet" by turning to another provider, obvious incentives exist for short-changing patients.

In a recent study with Anna Aizer and Enrico Moretti, I follow low-income women in California over time and look at the medical care that they received for births before and after they were required to join Medicaid managed care. The Medicaid mothers who were forced to join managed care organizations experienced delays in the initiation of prenatal care, went to lower-quality hospitals, and were more likely to have very low birth weight babies (babies less than 1,500 grams). Some of these babies died, and others were at risk for a lower future quality of life. Other studies of Medicaid managed care in California show that it increased, rather than decreased, costs. These results suggest that the gains derived from extending health insurance to low-income mothers decline if the quality of the care is undermined.[49] Hence stronger efforts should be made to monitor the quality of care provided under Medicaid managed care plans.

Summary

Research showing that lack of insurance coverage was a major problem for many American children prompted a tremendous effort to expand the safety net. It took more than fifteen years to implement fully the expansion of public health insurance coverage to all poor children, as well as to many children in families with somewhat higher income levels. These expansions reduced mortality and resulted in improvements in patterns of utilization of care. Still, the ongoing evaluation of this effort highlights several problems. Many of the newly eligible have not taken up their benefits and in some cases the insurance coverage and care provided under public health insurance programs is low quality.

The events of 2003 to 2005 show that the newly covered are vulnerable to cutbacks in state health insurance programs due to state fiscal crises. In 2003, Texas had dropped 160,000 children, about one-third of its SCHIP caseload, from the rolls and implemented a three-month waiting period before enrolled children can use medical services.

Colorado cut off prenatal care for illegal immigrant mothers in 2004, even though by law, their infants will be U.S. citizens. George Benjamin, executive director of the American Public Health Association, describes this as a "penny-wise, dollar-foolish policy [since] a small number of babies born with complications will wipe out any savings." Peter Leibig, director of a network of clinics serving poor women and children in Denver and Boulder, says that he will fight to provide care to those in need because "[i]f part of our mission is about breaking the cycle of poverty, we are not doing our mission by allowing more U.S. citizens to be born with disabilities and low weight." Government should make it easier, rather than harder, for people like Peter Leibig to do his job.[50]

In 2005, every state had either frozen or was considering freezing payments to doctors under the Medicaid program. In the most radical state move, Missouri plans to eliminate Medicaid altogether, refusing the federal subsidy in order to save money currently spent on the state matching grant component. The 2005 bill will eliminate health insurance for between 65,000 and 100,000 people. Donna Sevic, who worked at many low-wage jobs before she became crippled by arthritis, is one of them. Interviewed about the pending elimination of Medicaid she said, "If they take it away from me, I'll just go downhill. . . . I won't be here much longer. It's that plain and simple. . . . If you get out and try, really try to make a living, the government ought to step in and help you." Instead, the federal government is planning cutbacks to the Medicaid program that will force more states to make radical cutbacks in health insurance for the poor.[51]

The tragic irony of this situation is that cutting relatively healthy women and children off the roles will do very little to stem the tide of red ink in the Medicaid program. For example, work by Tom MaCurdy on Medi-Cal, the California Medicaid program, shows that the most expensive 5 percent of the cases incur 61 percent of the costs. These costs are overwhelmingly incurred by people who are elderly, blind, or disabled. The lowest-cost 75 percent of the caseload account for only 5 percent of Medicaid costs. Medicaid is really two different programs, one providing low-cost health care to families with children, and one providing high-cost care to the elderly and disabled. Cutting families off the rolls will do little to close the budget gap, but will cause significant hardship.[52]

Chapter 3

Feeding the Hungry: Food Stamps, School Nutrition Programs, and WIC

One in five Americans uses a federal food program every day. The creation of the food safety net began in earnest in 1946 with the creation of the National School Lunch Program. The nation was in shock over the large number of young men called up for World War II who were unfit for service because of nutrition-related deficiencies. By the age of twenty, many would-be draftees had already lost all their teeth, while others suffered from rickets, knock knees, or other skeletal deformations. In 1968, a group of physicians issued "Hunger in America," a landmark report documenting appalling levels of malnutrition among poor children. They wrote, "Wherever we went and wherever we looked, whether it was the rural south, Appalachia, or an urban ghetto, we saw children in significant numbers who were hungry and sick, children for whom hunger was a daily fact of life and sickness in many forms, an inevitability." Their report to Congress exposed levels of nutritional deficiencies in areas of the United States that were comparable to those in developing countries.[1]

This report was followed by a widening and deepening of the food safety net. The Food Stamp Program (FSP), which had begun as a small pilot in 1961, was greatly expanded over the next sixteen years. In 1971, national eligibility standards were established, and in 1974, states were required to extend the program statewide. WIC (the Special Supplemental Feeding Program for Women, Infants, and Children) was established in 1972 to provide nutritious food to pregnant women, infants, and preschool children. The National School Lunch Program (NLSP) was expanded, as was the School Breakfast Program (SBP), which had begun in 1966 as another pilot program. Ten years after their initial report rocked the nation, the doctors went back to areas like Appalachia and the inner cities. They found that while the poverty was still there, the widespread malnutrition was gone. The food safety net was in place and doing its job.

Fast forward to the present. In 2002, 34.9 million people in 12 million households lacked sufficient food for an active, healthy life for all household members. The U.S. Department of Agriculture calls this situation "food insecurity." Of these people, 9.4 million lived in households where people sometimes went hungry. One in ten households with incomes less than 185 percent of the poverty level experience hunger.[2] Faced with a shock to the household budget such as an unexpectedly high heating bill, many families are forced to cut back on food.[3] Do newspaper headlines about hungry children in America mean that the safety net put in place thirty years ago is failing?

Part of the answer is that the success of our food safety net programs has changed our conception of hunger. Instead of looking for children with skeletal deformities as a result of chronic malnutrition, we now look for households in which members worry about having enough food to eat or sometimes miss meals in their struggle to make ends meet. There is no denying that children still go hungry in America and that food insecurity has negative consequences. Food insecurity has been linked to higher levels of hyperactivity, absenteeism, aggression, and tardiness as well as impaired academic functioning among children.[4] More concretely, Jason DeParle describes visiting his subject Angie's house: "[I]t would sometimes be 9 p.m. and someone would be starting a fight in her house, and then I'd realize that part of it was that no one had eaten; they hadn't had dinner that evening."[5] But hunger of the severity documented in the "Hunger in America" report is now thankfully extremely rare, and shocking, when we do encounter it. To ignore the progress that has been made in eradicating hunger is to risk moving backward by allowing the safety net that many families depend on to be taken for granted.

A second puzzle is that while we continue to hear about hungry children, we are bombarded with stories about the "epidemic of obesity" in the United States. The 2001 Surgeon General's report shows that obesity has been rising more quickly among children than among adults, and that poor children are at greater risk than others. In the future, more children will die from complications of obesity than from smoking. A natural reaction is to conclude that children who are obese cannot be hungry.

Nutritionists, however, now argue that food insecurity and hunger may well be one of the causes of the obesity epidemic. In work with Jayanta Bhattacharya and Steven Haider, I show that in a national sample, poor, food-insecure teens are almost twice as likely to be obese as teens who are neither poor nor food insecure (18.1 compared to 10.8 percent). One study of homeless people in a New York City shelter found that 39 percent were obese. Families who wonder where their next meal is coming from are more likely to buy cheap foods that are high in fat and sugar, and less likely to buy expensive foods such as fruits and vegetables. Weight cycling due to periods of low food intake also contributes to obesity. Research by nutritionists at the University of Kentucky indicates that in households with food insecurity, participation in food safety net programs reduces the probability of obesity among adolescent girls.[6] The relationship between hunger and obesity means that it is more important than ever to ensure that safety net programs deliver nutritious foods rather than simply adding calories to the diet.

This chapter reviews the evidence regarding the effectiveness of the largest federal food and nutrition programs: the Food Stamp Program (FSP), the Supplemental Nutrition Program for Women, Infants, and Children (WIC) and the school nutrition programs. The variations in the characteristics of these programs, participation in them, and in their documented effects provide lessons about the types of food programs that help children in poor families most effectively.

The Food Stamp Program

In contrast to cash welfare, food stamp benefits are set at the national level, so that they help to provide a minimum, uniform, nationwide threshold for assistance. The FSP provides coupons (or, more recently, electronic debit cards) that can be redeemed for virtually anything edible other than alcohol, tobacco, hot foods intended for immediate consumption, and (paradoxically) vitamins.

Many families who are not eligible for cash welfare are eligible for food stamps. If a family is not automatically eligible because of participation in cash welfare, then they need to establish that they have "gross income" less than 130 percent of the federal poverty line, a "net income" less than poverty, and assets less than $2,000 (excluding the home and one car, as long as the car's value is less than $4,500). Gross income includes all cash income, while net income is income after allowing a standard deduction ($134 per month), a deduction for 20 percent of any earned income, and deductions for expenses such as child care (up to $200 per month), and shelter expenses to the extent that they exceed half of "countable" income (up to $250 per month).

Households on welfare are automatically eligible for the FSP. In these families, the FSP is designed to interact with cash welfare, so that it offsets state-level variation in the generosity of benefits. In a generous state like California, FSP benefits would add $187 to the TANF benefit of $626 per month for a family of four, bringing the total to $813, while in Texas, the FSP would add $314 to a TANF benefit of $201 for a total of $515.[7]

The Food Stamp Program is by far the largest federal food program, with 19.1 million recipients in 2002 and expenditures of 24.1 billion. The FSP is also the most similar to a cash welfare program because there are few restrictions on the types of food that can be purchased, and because the amount that most households receive in

FSP benefits is less than the amount of their food budgets. This means that the bulk of the FSP benefits is likely to be used to buy food that the household would have purchased in any case. The money saved by using the food stamps can then be spent on other things.

To see this, suppose that you were about to spend $100 on food in a grocery store, and you received a coupon entitling you to $50 off on your next purchase of groceries. Economic theory predicts that you would be glad to use the coupon, but that it would have relatively little impact on the composition of the goods in your basket. If the $50 coupon made you feel better off, you might buy some small luxuries that you would otherwise have foregone. If you typically spent only 15 cents of an extra dollar on food, then a dollar's worth of coupons would also increase your food spending by only 15 cents. That is, the $50 coupon would be expected to increase your total food purchases from $100 to $107.50. What this means is that only $7.50 of the $50 coupon would be used to purchase *additional* food. The rest of the coupon, $42.50 would simply displace money that would have been spent on food anyway. The money of your own that you did not spend on food would most likely be used to purchase nonfood items.

Several food stamp "cash-out" demonstrations have asked whether people actually treat food stamps the same as cash. In these experiments, households were issued checks instead of food stamps. The study with the cleanest design was carried out in San Diego. Some households receiving welfare payments and FSP benefits were randomly assigned either to a treatment group that received a check combining the two benefits, or to a control group that continued to receive FSP coupons separately. Surprisingly, the treatment group spent an average of $22 *less* per month on food, which suggests that giving people food coupons instead of cash really does increase their spending on food.

Diane Whitmore reexamined data from the San Diego experiment in order to figure out which households were spending less on food when they got cash instead of food stamps. What she shows is that some of the households in the treatment group were initially receiving food stamps worth more than what they wanted to spend on food. These households spent less on food after the cash-out. The majority of households received food stamps worth less than their food budgets and did treat them like cash. She finds that households that reduced spending in response to the "cash-out" program reduced spending on items like soda, and that these reductions had little effect on nutritional status.

Whitmore also provides evidence about food stamp trafficking and finds that food stamps sell for about 65 percent of their face value. The most recent study by the U.S. Department of Agriculture finds, though, that there is little trafficking in food stamps. The best estimate is that less than 2.5 cents on every dollar is lost to fraud. An interesting study of the issue found that often the same person both buys and sells food stamps within a month. This indicates that some households are so short of cash that they budget on a day-to-day basis rather than a monthly basis. The value of the monthly FSP benefits that they receive is more than what is needed for the next few days, and so they sell the remainder to buy other necessities. Then, if additional cash comes into the household later in the month, they purchase more food stamps to stretch their food budgets. One way to solve this problem would be to credit the benefits to recipients' cards at weekly rather than monthly intervals.[8]

Whitmore's findings cast doubt on the hypothesis that, on average, households with children treat food stamps any differently than cash. It is possible, though, that some subset of these households benefits from receiving the stamps rather than cash. Female heads of household may have more control over the use of FSP benefits than they have over cash income, given that many female heads live with partners.[9] In these households, the fact that food stamps are issued in the woman's name and ear-marked for food purchases may increase her ability to spend the income on food.

Many studies have examined the effects of the FSP on food purchases and intakes of specific nutrients, while only a few studies have looked at the effects of the FSP on food insecurity or other outcomes. Typically, studies compare eligible participants to eligible nonparticipants and try to control statistically for observed differences between the two types of households. The main problem with this exercise is that participants may differ from eligible nonparticipants in ways that are not observed by the researcher. As a result, some studies find that the FSP actually *reduces* consumption of some important nutrients.[10] It is hard to imagine how giving people food coupons or debit cards could do this. A more plausible explanation is that people who participate in FSP are often less likely to eat a healthy diet for reasons that have nothing to do with the program.

It is clear that the FSP has not eliminated nutritional problems. The National FSP Survey of 1996 found that 50 percent of FSP participants experienced food insecurity and substantial numbers of FSP recipients fell short of the recommended daily allowances for important nutrients—31 percent of FSP households were short of iron, while 21 percent were short of folate, which comes primarily from green leafy vegetables. At the same time, FSP participants are more likely to be obese.[11] One problem is that, as discussed earlier, FSP participants are free to buy foods of little nutritional value.

Still, it is possible that the FSP makes families better off nutritionally than they would be otherwise.[12] FSP families do spend more on food than other similar families, with most estimates suggesting that an additional dollar of food stamps leads to an increase in food expenditures of between \$.17 and \$.47. These estimates imply that there is a lot of leakage in this "bucket" of aid, since much of the money freed up by FSP is spent on other goods. Still, these increases in expenditures do seem to be associated with increases in the nutrient content of food purchased by the household. A careful study by Barbara Devaney and Robert Moffitt found that the FSP increased consumption of calories, protein, vitamin A, vitamin B6, vitamin C, thiamin, riboflavin, calcium, iron, magnesium, and phosphorus. And several studies have shown increases in nutrient intakes among preschool children on the FSP.[13]

It is hard to know how these increases in consumption translate into nutritional benefits. If families were short of specific nutrients, then moving them toward the U.S. recommended daily allowances would be an achievement; while if most people are meeting or exceeding these allowances (as they certainly are for calories, protein, and some vitamins), then increasing their consumption could even be harmful. What we would like to know is whether the FSP increases the consumption of households who are not meeting their daily allowances for specific nutrients, and how it affects the composition of the diet.

Judged even by this strict criterion, the FSP appears to have some positive effects. Peter Basiotis and colleagues find that FSP participants have healthier diets than nonparticipants. In work with Jayanta Bhattacharya, we show that, controlling for characteristics such as age, education, race, and household structure, teenage FSP participants are less likely to be food insecure. Similarly, David Rose and colleagues have found that the incidence of food insecurity decreases with the size of the FSP benefit that a household is eligible to receive.[14]

The FSP can teach us much about why needy families don't always take up the benefits they are entitled to. In 1994, when FSP enrollments were at their peak, only 69 percent of eligible individuals were enrolled. Determining eligibility is complicated since becoming certified requires people to document the value of their assets, earnings, and expenses. In 1999, the average new FSP application took nearly five hours of time to complete, including at least two trips to the welfare office. Recertification for benefits took 2.5 hours and at least one trip. Out-of-pocket application costs averaged about $10.31 or 6 percent of the average monthly benefit.[15]

A 2000 survey of state practices found that most applications were at least ten pages long and included warnings of a stiff fine and jail time for people submitting misleading answers. In twenty-nine states, the forms then go on to ask people applying for food stamps if they own a prepaid burial plot. If they do, they are required to document its value. This macabre provision is apparently in response to an obscure federal regulation that allows families to exclude only one grave per customer when estimating the value of a family's assets. In Nevada and Nebraska, applicants are asked if they sell their blood, and how much they get for it.

In South Dakota, applicants are required to document any bingo winnings. In Ohio, applicants are asked, "Are you or anyone in your household fleeing from New Jersey?" This bizarre provision was added in response to federal regulations that prohibit food stamps for fugitives from prosecution of a felony. In New Jersey, felonies are called "high misdemeanors," and so a separate question was added to the Ohio form just to cover this contingency![16]

Families seeking to maintain their eligibility must go through this whole process at frequent intervals. The standard interval is every six months. Ironically, working families may be required to come back to the welfare office every three months, because their incomes are more variable than the incomes of households on public assistance. In principal, families on the FSP are supposed to report any changes in their income to the welfare office, which could entail reassessment of eligibility at even more frequent intervals. In work with Jeffrey Grogger, I have shown that the length of the recertification interval has a significant effect on participation in the program—the more often people are required to jump through all these hoops, the less likely they are to take up their benefits, even if they continue to need them.

We also examined the effect of switching from coupons to electronic debit cards, as all states were required to do by 2002. People often talk about the "stigma" associated with using food stamps. Using bulky paper coupons to pay for one's groceries might well prove embarrassing, and shame could prevent people from using the program. If this were the case, then one might expect the move to a discrete debit card to increase participation. We did not find any evidence of this however, suggesting that the direct costs of signing up for the program may be a more important barrier to participation than shame.[17]

Another reason why people might not sign up for the FSP is that they don't know that they are eligible. In an interesting study to test this idea, Beth Daponte, Seth Sanders, and Lowell Taylor ran an experiment in which they contacted households and told them how much they were eligible for in terms of food stamp benefits. They found that households that were contacted were more likely than other households to take up the benefits, but that those with larger benefits were much more likely to participate than those with smaller benefits. If lack of information were the only problem preventing participation, then one would expect people with large and small benefits to be equally likely to sign up. Hence, their result indicates that people find it costly to participate in the FSP, and will only do it if the benefit exceeds the cost.[18]

Since making it harder for people to enroll reduces the probability that they participate, it is not surprising that welfare reform had a large effect on participation in the FSP. Families leaving the welfare rolls generally remained eligible for the FSP, but lost their automatic eligibility, so that they had to go through an onerous enrollment process to remain on the rolls. Participation in the FSP hovered around 20 million persons per year during the 1980s, but rose sharply in the early 1990s to a peak of approximately 27 million persons in 1994. Aaron Yelowitz provides evidence that this run-up in the FSP caseload was partly caused by expansions of the Medicaid program. Families that did not find it worthwhile to sign up for food stamps became more likely to participate when a trip to the welfare office could result in certification for both food stamps and Medicaid.[19] Conversely, FSP participation fell sharply following welfare reform to 20.8 million participants by 1998.

Just as there is strong debate about how much of the decline in the welfare rolls can be attributed to welfare reform, there is debate about how much of the decline in FSP participation is due to the strong economy of the early 1990s rather than to welfare reform. If one examines the FSP caseload as a percentage of the population that is in poverty, one also sees an increase followed by a decline. In 1995, 48.6 percent of the population with incomes less than 130 percent of the poverty line participated in the FSP compared to only 38.9 percent of this population in 1998. The fraction of FSP households with children and single heads also fell dramatically from 50 to 39.6 percent between 1995 and 1998.

A study by the Urban Institute found that families who left welfare were more likely to leave the FSP than other similar families, and that the difference was greatest at the lowest income levels.

What this suggests is that welfare reform caused people to lose food stamps not because their incomes went up, but because these poor families had a hard time reestablishing their eligibility for the benefits. Estimates of the extent of the decline in FSP that can be attributed to good economic conditions range from 28 to 44 percent, suggesting a large role for welfare reform.[20]

Along with welfare reform, many observers cite a hostile climate in welfare offices. In California, New York, and Texas, food stamp applicants are fingerprinted in an effort to reduce fraud. This requirement may be eliminated in California, because a state audit revealed that the costs of the program ($31 million for implementation and $8.5 million to operate it each year) were much higher than the cost of the fraud prevented.[21]

Despite repeated efforts to improve access to the program in New York City, a September 2003 undercover investigation found that 11 percent of the sites listed by the city's Human Resource Administration as food stamp offices did not exist; that investigators were not able to obtain an application for the FSP from the existing sites a quarter of the time; that 27 percent of these sites did not have any written information about the program available on site; and that 52 percent of the time applicants were illegally asked personal information while attempting to get an application. Since the FSP is a federal program, it is not in the interest of city or state welfare agencies to make it difficult for people to enroll, which is why New York City conducted this investigation. The hostility and misinformation found by the New York investigators are just one example of the barriers to accessing safety net programs faced by the poor.[22]

We have seen that the FSP is very similar to cash welfare in that families treat the benefits much like cash. The FSP resembles the old AFDC program in another respect, since it also penalizes households for work.[23] For every dollar that an FSP family earns, it loses $.30 in FSP benefits. Under certain circumstances, households may face even larger losses. For example, in 1998, the gross income limit for a family of three was $1,445, while the maximum food stamp allotment was $321 per month. If the household earned

$1,446, they would be ineligible for food stamps because of the gross income limit. If they earned $1,444, then they would remain eligible. If they took the deduction for one child, and had excess shelter expenses of $200, then they would qualify for a benefit of $127 per month. Thus, by earning $2 more per month, the household would lose $127, for a net loss of $125! Even a family with a very strong work ethic could be discouraged from working by penalties of this magnitude.

Households are also "taxed" on their welfare payments. For every dollar that a state transfers in the form of TANF benefits, the federal government reduces FSP transfers by $.30. Fortunately, households are not penalized for receiving the EITC—it does not count as income in determining eligibility for programs such as the FSP. Because the EITC and other in-kind benefits are not counted in determining eligibility for federal programs, families will be better off receiving these benefits than receiving cash assistance from states.

WIC

If the FSP is similar to cash, then the WIC program is at the opposite end of the spectrum.[24] WIC offers coupons that can be redeemed only for specific types of food by eligible women and children who are certified to be at nutritional risk. These foods are chosen to meet the nutritional needs of the caseload of pregnant and nursing women, infants, and children under five. If you go into a supermarket in a poor area, you will likely see notices on store shelves about which foods can be purchased using WIC coupons. The included foods are good sources of protein, iron, calcium, and vitamins A and C. The monthly value of WIC benefits is small compared to food stamps—in 1994 it varied from $40.49 in the Southeast to $52.68 in the West. WIC also involves a nutrition education component, which women receive when they go in to pick up the food coupons.

Participants are offered nutritional counseling at each visit and must be certified to be at nutritional risk. In practice no one is turned away for failing to meet the nutritional risk criteria. This is partly because there are many different risks (e.g. anemia, obesity, and improper diet). I served on a National Research Council examining eligibility and participation in the WIC program, and we concluded that all of the experts on the panel had some nutritional risk factors! This is less surprising if you consider that current nutritional guidelines state that everyone should have five servings of fruits and vegetables per day and that few Americans meet this requirement. WIC agencies are also required to help participants obtain preventive health care either by providing services onsite or through referrals.

In 2002, WIC served 7.5 million people a month at an annual cost of $4.4 billion. The income cutoff for WIC is set higher than for the FSP, at 185 percent of the federal poverty line. Women and children who participate in Medicaid are automatically eligible even if their incomes exceed the 185 percent cutoff. The recent expansions of the Medicaid income cutoffs for pregnant women, infants, and children mean that many people with incomes above 185 percent of poverty are now eligible. Douglas Besharov and Peter Germanis criticize this largely unintended expansion of the WIC program to people of higher income, although Marianne Bitler, John Karl Scholz, and I find little evidence that people with incomes above 185 percent of poverty are taking up the program in large numbers.[25]

We find that in any given month of 1998, 58 percent of all infants were eligible for WIC. Roughly 45 percent received WIC benefits, so that the take-up rate among eligible infants was 73.2 percent. Among children ages one to four, 57 percent were eligible for WIC, and 38 percent of eligible children received benefits. Estimates for pregnant and postpartum women are less accurate, since most surveys don't collect information about breastfeeding, but we estimate that 54 percent of all pregnant and postpartum women are eligible for WIC and that 66.5 percent of these women received benefits.

In contrast to the FSP, where an extensive effort is made to monitor individual compliance with eligibility standards through a federally mandated quality control system, there is no federally co-ordinated attempt to eliminate fraud in WIC at the individual level. We estimate, however, that of the infants receiving WIC in any given month in 1998, only 5.9 percent were ineligible for the benefits. Similarly, of the 3.7 million children receiving benefits, 5.4 percent did not meet the eligibility criteria and had not done so for the past six months. These error rates are consistent with those reported in the 2001 National Survey of WIC Participants. On the whole then, WIC is well targeted to the pregnant women and children it is intended to serve.

These estimates were produced against a background of Congressional concern about high rates of participation in the WIC program. Official government estimates of the number of participating infants were greater than estimates of the number of eligible infants, so that the official participation rate in the late 1990s was over 100 percent! The National Research Council Panel, charged with looking into the matter, concluded that official estimates of the number of eligible infants and children were much too low, since they did not take into account children who were eligible because of their participation in the Medicaid program. The official estimates also ignored the fact that people could become eligible for WIC due to low income in a given month, and then remain certified for a fixed period without violating program rules. The panel's interim report, issued in 2001, put a speedy end to allegations of massive fraud within the WIC program.[26]

WIC is the most studied federal food program, and the evidence shows that "WIC Works." In 1992, the U.S. General Accounting Office (GAO) reviewed seventeen studies of the effects of prenatal WIC participation on newborns. All seventeen found that WIC participation reduced the incidence of low birth weight (birth weight less than 2,500 grams) by between 10 and 43 percent, and that it reduced the incidence of very low birth weight (less than 1,500 grams) between 21 and 53 percent. These numbers represent huge improvements in the health of newborns. According to the GAO, providing WIC services to mothers of babies born in 1990 saved federal tax payers more than $337 million in medical costs. They conclude that a dollar invested in WIC saves at least $3.50 in other costs. Since the GAO evaluation, many other studies have reported similar positive findings.[27]

Dr. Jean Mayer, a noted expert on nutrition and former President of Tufts University, explains the cost savings this way:

> Women who are not fed properly during pregnancy have about 30 to 40 percent more low birth weight infants. It costs one to two thousand dollars a day to keep an underweight infant in an incubator. You can buy a lot of food for that, and you can see how not feeding pregnant women can be extraordinarily expensive. Infants born underweight are also more likely to have physical defects or to be mentally retarded. In Massachusetts, for instance, the lifetime cost of maintaining a retarded person is $2.5 million. It can be said—forgetting all humanitarian considerations, on financial terms alone—that one of the stupidest ways to try to save money is not to feed pregnant women."[28]

Dr. Mayer's comments not withstanding, economists like myself are trained to raise questions about these types of estimates. It is always difficult to tell if a program works simply by comparing participants and nonparticipants. The two groups are likely to differ, both in terms of things that can be observed, like income, and in terms of things that are more difficult to observe, like motivation. If mothers who signed up for WIC were more motivated to eat properly than other mothers, then perhaps they would have had healthier babies even without the program. This is the point of a review of WIC studies by Douglas Besharov and Peter Rossi, who argue (correctly) that the most convincing way to test for whether WIC is or is not effective would be to conduct a large-scale experimental study with randomly chosen treatments and controls.[29] It would be difficult, however, to conduct such a study if it involved randomly denying benefits to women and children who currently receive them.

Direct investigation of the question of how WIC mothers differ from other mothers should put some of these concerns about selection to rest because it shows that WIC mothers are much more disadvantaged than other mothers. In work with Marianne Bitler, I examine detailed information about women whose deliveries were paid for by Medicaid and find that those on WIC were worse off in every observable dimension than those who were not. The WIC mothers were more likely to be obese, more likely to smoke, less likely to have a bathroom in their residence, and less likely to have a husband or partner present at the birth. Nancy Burstein found that WIC mothers scored lower on a test of coping skills than other low-income mothers. If anything then, the WIC mothers would be expected to have less healthy babies than other mothers, which makes the finding of positive WIC effects all the more remarkable. One especially notable study by Lori Kowaleski-Jones and Greg Duncan examines sibling pairs in which one sib participated in WIC and the other did not, and finds that participation in WIC increases birth weight by 7 ounces. Comparing siblings offers a powerful way to control for common aspects of family background.[30]

While the provision of WIC to pregnant women is a great success story, the effects of WIC on infants and children are less well studied. One downside to WIC is that it discourages breast-feeding.[31] Breast milk is universally acknowledged to be the best food for infants, and the American Academy of Pediatrics recommends that infants be exclusively breast-fed for the first six months. Breast-feeding is associated with higher IQ scores, as well as reductions in illnesses such as ear infections and asthma. But breast-feeding can be difficult. Despite the fact that breast milk is a "natural" food, it is not uncommon to face problems such as infants who don't know how to nurse—and mothers are not born knowing how to breast-feed their infants. Women who were formula-fed themselves, and whose friends and acquaintances use formula, have difficulty finding anyone to teach them. The result is that many mothers who initiate breast-feeding quickly give it up and turn to formula.

WIC gives free formula to mothers who choose not to breast-feed. State WIC agencies get a manufacturers' rebate for each can of formula that WIC participants "purchase" using their vouchers. These WIC "sales" account for 50 percent of the formula purchased in the United States. In return for the rebates, formula manufacturers get exclusive sales agreements with the state. That is, WIC participants receive vouchers that can be redeemed only for a particular brand of formula, making the manufacturer of that brand the sole supplier to the WIC market in the state. In fiscal year 2002, infant formula accounted for around 46 percent of total WIC food costs on a pre-rebate basis but only 21 percent on a post-rebate basis. State WIC agencies depend on the additional revenues from these rebates to finance parts of their WIC programs.[32]

Since formula is expensive, the free formula provided by WIC removes a powerful incentive for women to nurse their babies. Even without this incentive, WIC mothers are less likely than other mothers to breast-feed because women who are young, poor, African American, or less educated are less likely to nurse their babies. Moreover, those readers who have tried it will understand that pumping breast milk to accommodate a work schedule is neither pleasant nor convenient, and so it is hardly surprising that working mothers are less likely to breast-feed. Although WIC centers are required to teach pregnant women that "breast is best," the net effect of WIC on breast-feeding has been negative.

A simple solution to this problem would be to make it more difficult for women to receive formula rather than to breast-feed. Such a policy could back-fire, however, because if women are not going to nurse their babies in any case, then WIC at least insures that the babies get proper formula and infant cereal. Giving women free formula has been shown to delay the introduction of cow's milk (which is not recommended before one year), and of solid foods (which are not recommended before four months). Instead of making it difficult for women to get formula, WIC agencies have intensified efforts to encourage breast-feeding in recent years. For example, agencies now give nursing mothers benefits that are of similar value to those that include expensive formula. Work by Pinka Chatterji and Jeanne Brooks-Gunn indicates that these efforts may be paying off, since they do not find any negative effect of WIC on breast-feeding in their study using data from 1999 and 2000.[33]

WIC increases the consumption of the target nutrients that are included in the foods WIC participants are allowed to purchase.

David Rose, Jean-Pierre Habicht, and Barbara Devaney find that WIC has positive effects on the consumption of protein, vitamin B6, vitamin E, folate, thiamin, riboflavin, niacin, iron, magnesium, and zinc. WIC has been credited with a dramatic decline in the incidence of anemia among young children that took place between 1975 and 1985. The prevalence of anemia fell from 7.8 to 2.9 percent over this short period, while WIC grew rapidly to the point that by 1980, half of all infants born in the United States were participating. Studies indicate that these improvements in nutrition affect children's behavior and ability to learn. Children on WIC prenatally have been found to have higher scores on the Peabody Picture Vocabulary Test, which is a good predictor of future scholastic achievement.[34]

Many children eat too much food rather than too little, and so recent studies have investigated the relationship between WIC and the risk of overweight. A 1996 Centers for Disease Control study finds that children on WIC are as likely to be obese as other children. It is hard to tell, however, what the effect of WIC is from these kinds of comparisons. If the children who were on WIC were more likely to be overweight than other children to begin with (perhaps because of poor diets at home), then a program that brought the risk of obesity down to the same level as other children would have to be considered a success. It is important to try to determine how the WIC kids would have done in the absence of the program.

In recent work with Marianne Bitler, we focus on children who became eligible for WIC because of expansions in the Medicaid program. The idea is to compare poor children who were ineligible for WIC to children who are the same in terms of income and family background, but who became eligible because of the Medicaid expansions. We find that children who joined WIC because of changes in Medicaid program were less likely than similar children to be overweight at age four.[35]

Like the FSP, WIC yields important clues about the causes of nonparticipation. Given the dire consequences of poor nutrition in pregnancy and early childhood, why don't all eligible families participate? For many families the answer may be that the time and energy needed to apply are not worth the benefits. Marianne Bitler, Karl Scholz, and I show that requiring people to pick up their coupons more often reduces participation. Nancy Burstein and her collaborators show that WIC participation falls off steeply at children's first birthdays. One reason is that the benefits become less valuable, since they no longer allow women to purchase infant formula, but another reason is that the child must become recertified at this point.

Recently, concern has been expressed about the "WIC only" stores that cater to people with WIC coupons by making it easy to find the WIC items and also treating these customers with consideration and respect. Unfortunately, these stores have also been charging higher prices (though this was addressed in 2004 legislation reauthorizing the WIC program). People use them because while the prices in supermarkets may be lower, "it's often a hassle finding the right products and dealing with cashiers."[36]

Unlike the FSP, which has always been fully funded, WIC is funded by Congressional appropriation. If the funds are not adequate to serve all eligible women and children, then states will be forced to use waiting lists. For many years, WIC was funded at levels high enough that there were no waiting lists, but in recent years, waiting lists have reemerged as a barrier to participation. For instance, the state budget crisis in Minnesota meant cutbacks for WIC. In 2003, some women were driving fifty miles to receive WIC vouchers, and waiting lists were increasing. In March 2004, there were waiting lists not only for children but also for pregnant women in Boise, Idaho.[37]

School Nutrition Programs

School nutrition programs fall between WIC and the FSP in terms of expenditures, the extent to which they target particular groups, and the emphasis on supplying only nutritious foods. School nutrition programs provide free or reduced price meals to low-income children in schools. The meals must conform to the Dietary Guidelines for Americans by not only providing one-third of the recommended dietary allowances of various nutrients, but also by limiting intakes of fat, saturated fat, sodium, and cholesterol, and by providing plenty of vegetables, fruits, grains, and dietary fiber. Like the FSP, both the National School Lunch Program and the School Breakfast Program are entitlement programs, which means that every eligible person must be served. Almost all public schools participate in the lunch program, and about four out of five schools that offer lunch also offer a school breakfast. Every day, 6.7 million children receive a free or reduced-price school breakfast, while 16 million receive a free or reduced-price school lunch.

School meals programs work by reimbursing schools for the meals that are served. Children with incomes less than 130 percent of poverty (the same cutoff as the FSP) are eligible to receive free meals, and the school gets reimbursed $2.19 for each lunch, and $1.17 for each breakfast; children with incomes between 130 and 185 percent of poverty (the cutoffs for the FSP and WIC) can be charged no more than $.40 for lunch and $.30 for breakfast. Schools get reimbursed $1.79 for each reduced price lunch and $.87 for each reduced price breakfast. Schools can be reimbursed a small amount ($.22 per meal) for serving students with incomes higher than these cutoffs. Schools also receive commodity aid—in 2003–2004 this aid averaged about 15.75 cents per meal. The commodity aid reflects the programs' roots as a way to dispose of surplus agricultural commodities but is a small fraction of total aid at this point.[38]

Unlike the FSP, which can be used to purchase even junk food, school meals must follow government-approved meal plans. Since 1995, meals have been required to follow the *Dietary Guidelines for Americans* as discussed earlier. Critics from the Left and Right have roundly criticized school meals for failing to live up to this standard. For example, the Physicians Committee for Responsible Medicine, which promotes vegan and vegetarian diets, says that school lunches are failing our children and gives most of the school lunches they have rated a grade between C and F. Douglas Besharov of the

American Enterprise Institute claims that "the levels of fat and saturated fat in school lunches exceed the lunch program's own standards by about 10 percent. Successive administrations have tried to reduce the fat content of the meals, but with only modest success."[39]

The government's own studies paint a more positive picture. School meals provide the vitamins and minerals that children need for a healthy diet, and while many schools fail to meet the targets for fat and saturated fat, they are much closer now than they were before the new standards were implemented. The guidelines say that a maximum of 30 percent of calories can come from fat, and a maximum of 10 percent of calories can come from saturated fats. On average, in 1998–99, 33 percent of the calories in school lunches came from fat and 12 percent came from saturated fat. Compared to 1991–92, these levels represent a reduction of about 10 percent in calories from fat and 22 percent in calories from saturated fat. School breakfasts were close to meeting the guidelines in 1991–92, and most breakfasts were in compliance with the guidelines by 1998–99—the average percentages of calories from fat and saturated fats in elementary school breakfasts were 25.8 and 9.8 percent respectively.[40]

School meals are held to high standards, as they should be—and most schools are making progress in meeting these standards. Critics of school nutrition programs suggest that fat-laden meals at school lead to a lifetime of obesity. Yet many American children at all income levels have diets that fall far short of the Dietary Guidelines for Americans; and the food in school meals is often significantly better than the food children would eat otherwise. For some children, the programs are a necessity. Rebecca Skeens, an assistant principal in rural Virginia, knows children who don't eat for days when school is closed over a long weekend.[41]

The most recent comprehensive study of the nutrition of children who eat school meals is based on data collected in 1991–1992, before the new dietary guidelines went into effect. These data show that the average child who ate school lunch on the day he or she was surveyed ate the same number of calories as the average child who did not. Since weight depends on the number of calories consumed (and expended) this result suggests that school meals do not make children obese. School lunches generally met or exceeded the goal of providing one-third of the recommended daily allowances for all vitamins and minerals and increased children's intakes of protein, vitamin A, vitamin B12, riboflavin, calcium, phosphorus, magnesium, and zinc. Lunch participants consumed more milk, meat or meat substitutes, and vegetables at lunch than did nonparticipants. Nonparticipants were more likely to be short of vitamin A, vitamin B6, calcium, iron, and zinc. Intakes of fat and sodium were higher in the school lunch group, though recent progress in reducing fat and salt in school meals suggests that this may not be true today.[42] Diane Whitmore has analyzed data on kindergarten and first graders that was collected in 1995–96, right around the time that the new meal guidelines came in, as well as data from a national survey conducted between 1988 and 1994 (before the new guidelines). Her work suggests that students who started out at the same weight as other students but ate school lunch in kindergarten were about two percentage points more likely to be overweight in first grade. Again, it is not known how much movement toward compliance with the new standards has improved this situation.[43]

In work with Jayanta Bhattacharya using data from the same period, he and I try to identify the causal effect of school lunch by comparing children measured while school was in session to children measured during the summer, when schools were closed. To account for seasonal differences in nutrition, we do this comparison both for children who were eligible for school meals and for those who were not. We then look at whether the availability of school lunch changes nutrient intakes more for the eligible children than for the ineligible ones. We find that the availability of school lunch reduces the fraction of adolescents with high blood cholesterol and improves the quality of their diets.[44]

Research on the School Breakfast Program also shows that it improves children's nutrition. It increases the consumption of vitamins and minerals and reduces the percentage of calories from fat.

Studies have examined the impact of school breakfast on children's academic achievement by measuring the same children before and after school breakfast became available at their schools. These studies find that school breakfast improves both attendance and test scores.[45]

A study by Sandra Hofferth and Sally Curtin uses data from the 1997 Panel Study of Income Dynamics (collected after the new guidelines went into effect) and finds no evidence that school nutrition programs contributed to being overweight when differences between families and children were accounted for. They also find that it is near-poor and working-class children who are at greatest risk of being overweight, rather than poor children, which may provide some evidence of a protective effect of the food safety net.[46]

Just as WIC was attacked for supposedly serving large numbers of ineligible children, critics have attacked school meal programs for serving ineligible children. In the run-up to the 2004 reauthorization of the child nutrition programs, the Bush administration argued that many ineligible children had been certified as eligible for free or reduced-price school meals. The administration advocated increasing the amount of income-checking to reduce the amount of fraud in the program and "ensure program integrity." On the other side of the debate, advocacy groups such as the Food Research and Action Committee (FRAC) argued that many eligible children were not being served. For example, less than half of the children who ate school lunch also ate school breakfast although if they were eligible for lunch, they would also be eligible for breakfast.[47]

Parents receive an application for the school meals program at the beginning of the year. They are asked to fill in the incomes of all household members, but are not required to submit proof of income. Schools are then required to select about three percent of applications for income verification, and the selected parents must submit documentation of their income by a given date. Otherwise, their children are cut off. This practice of relying on the "honor system" for reporting income and then checking some applicants is similar to the way in which the government deals with income taxes.

Parents whose incomes rise by more than $50 a month are required to notify the school district so that their eligibility for school meals can be reassessed. In practice though, this requirement has never been enforced.

A pilot study in several school districts investigated the effects of increasing verification procedures as the administration had proposed. In one scheme, all households were required to submit income documents along with their application forms. In another scheme, a higher fraction of households were selected to have their income verified. Surprisingly, these measures increased administrative costs but had no effect on the probability that ineligible families were certified to receive free or reduced price meals. The stricter requirements did, however, discourage eligible families from applying.

These measures had little effect on participation by ineligible families, because most families accurately report their income on the application. Some of these families are then found to be ineligible at the time that income is verified, because school districts mistakenly signed them up, or because their income has changed. Low-income families tend to have unstable income. It is not uncommon for families with annual incomes below the poverty line to have a month or two during the year in which their income is above the poverty line. Hence, a family that is certified to receive benefits in September could be ineligible for benefits when they are checked in December, but become eligible again in January. Such a family is unlikely to be headed by a Cadillac-driving welfare queen. The family remains needy throughout the year but is simply slightly less needy in some months than in others.

Half of the households that are asked to document income don't respond by the deadline, and so their children are cut off. It is tempting to assume that they did not respond because they were really not eligible; but a government study found that 77 percent of free-meal families who did not respond were actually eligible for either free or reduced price meals. Among households that did respond, only 16 percent were found to be ineligible for free or reduced-price meals. This study shows that while there are ineligible children receiving benefits, measures designed to catch these children also discourage large numbers of eligible children from participation in the program.

A second study shows that as many as a third of children eligible for subsidized meals are never certified to receive them. These studies show that if everyone was correctly certified and receiving the benefits they were entitled to, program costs would go up rather than down. In other words, nonparticipation by eligibles is a much bigger problem than participation by ineligibles. In the face of the evidence, proposals to increase verification requirements have been shelved, at least temporarily. As Representative George Miller said, "While I support efforts to control inappropriate use of the program, the cure should not be worse than the disease."[48]

Recent Legislation

The Child Nutrition and WIC Reauthorization Act of 2004 adopted several measures that make it easier for children to qualify for school nutrition programs. First, the measure makes children eligible for the entire year, and allows families to fill in a single application for all the children in the household. The U.S. Department of Agriculture, which administers these programs, had suggested full-year eligibility. This change eliminates the largely unenforced (and unenforceable) requirement that families report small changes in their income to their schools. Another reform, backed by Senator Elizabeth Dole, would have eliminated the "reduced-price" category and made all children with incomes less than 185 percent of poverty eligible for free meals. The 2004 Act allowed five states to do this on a trial basis, if there is enough funding.[49]

Funding will be a key issue in future years. The 2004 Act continued funding at current levels for 2005. But language buried deep in budget documents suggests that food and nutrition programs will be cut in future years. If we stay on the current collision course between federal government revenues and federal government spending, cuts in programs like these will be inevitable.

The act made "direct certification" of households on food stamps mandatory. The income cutoffs for food stamps and school meals are the same. Under direct certification, the fact that the family is eligible for food stamps is used to show that they are also eligible for school meals. The family is not required to complete an additional application. While many school districts already used direct certification prior to 2004, about 35 percent did not. Direct certification has been shown to increase the participation of eligible children, and it is easy to see why: Surveys of eligible nonparticipants indicate that over half of them believe that they are not eligible, 10 percent think that the certification procedure is difficult, and 20 percent find the application procedure stigmatizing. Steps to simplify application procedures should have large impacts on participation. Other provisions of the 2004 reauthorization act allow migrant, homeless, and run-away children to receive free school meals, and make it easier for the children of military families to qualify.[50]

Other Concerns

This chapter has so far neglected several smaller food programs. One of the most important is the Child and Adult Care Food Program, which operates somewhat like the school meals programs, but serves approximately 1.7 million low-income children in daycare centers. The Summer Service Program serves meals in some poor areas during the summer, when children do not get school meals. When it is operating, the program serves about 2.3 million children per day. There has been little investigation of the benefits of participation in these programs, but the positive effects of the school meal programs suggest that providing meals to younger children, and during summer vacation, makes sense.

The discussion so far has also neglected two "big picture" questions raised in previous chapters: Whether the nutrition programs discourage people from working, and whether they discourage people from marrying. In principal, any program that provides a valuable benefit to people with low incomes may discourage them from working harder to increase their incomes. Yet direct studies of the extent to which nutrition programs reduce the work effort of single mothers suggest that these effects are small. Effects on the labor supply of married couples are even smaller. Given these small effects, we should be asking ourselves, along with Representative Miller, whether the "cure" of slashing the safety net to make people work harder would not be worse than the "disease."[51]

The food safety net programs treat couples that live together the same as married people. This is quite different than cash welfare or the EITC. According to the FSP, a household is a group of people who share income to buy food, and who prepare meals together. WIC generally takes a similar view (though caseworkers have a great deal of flexibility), and application forms for the school meal programs ask about the income of all of the adults in the household without specifying that any of them need to be married to each other. This means that there are no "marriage penalties" in the food programs, which raises the question of whether this principal could be extended to other programs?

Summary

The food safety net works. Over the past thirty-five years, it has helped eliminate the worst forms of hunger and malnutrition in the United States. Still, the individual programs could all be improved. Food stamps appear to be less effective at improving nutrition than WIC, in part because they can be used to buy junk food. Food stamp benefits should be restricted to the purchase of nutritious foods. Now that we use debit cards rather than cumbersome stamps, FSP trafficking could be reduced by crediting benefits to people's cards in weekly rather than monthly increments. (The introduction of a debit card per se does not eliminate trafficking, since people can let others use their debit cards for a fee). On the other hand, efforts to reduce fraud through measures like fingerprinting must be reevaluated. The evidence suggests that the money spent on fingerprinting exceeds the value of any savings to the program through fraud that is prevented, and fingerprinting discourages needy people from using food stamps. State and federal governments should also take a hard look at reforming the process of determining eligibility, by removing questions about things like burial plots, blood donations, and bingo winnings.

A major problem with WIC is that it is not an entitlement program. There is a real risk that the funds set aside for WIC will not keep up with increases in demand among poor women and children. While WIC has very positive effects overall, it has discouraged breast-feeding. This is an important problem given the large fraction of WIC dollars spent on formula, and the positive effects of nursing. Efforts to encourage breast-feeding need to be evaluated so that best practices can be universally adopted. WIC benefits for pregnant women and children should also be amended to include more fresh fruits and vegetables, as a report from the National Academy's Institute of Medicine has recently recommended.[52]

The school meals programs need to continue working to meet the Dietary Guidelines for Americans. Even so, it is important to keep in mind that school meals are generally healthier than the meals that children would eat in the absence of the program. Adopting full-year certification and direct certification will improve the accuracy of certification procedures without discouraging eligible children from using the programs.

This chapter also highlights some more global problems with food and nutrition programs. First, large numbers of eligible people do not receive benefits. Lack of participation by eligibles has been shown to be a much more important problem than participation by a small number of people who aren't eligible. It requires great effort to negotiate the maze of programs, all with different eligibility requirements. Also, maintaining eligibility is onerous. It makes little sense to penalize working families by making them come to the welfare office more frequently than other people in order to maintain their benefits. The patchwork of programs and lack of coordination between them increases administrative costs by requiring that people be evaluated many times. Streamlining and increasing coordination between food and nutrition programs (as well as other safety net programs) could increase take-up and reduce costs, ensuring that more needy people are served for the same budget. This theme is taken up and expanded on in chapter 6.

Chapter 4

Home Sweet Home?

For some, the words "public housing" conjure indelible images of horrific crimes. In October 1992, seven-year-old Dantrell Davis was walking to school holding his mother's hand when he was shot in the face by a sniper in Chicago's notorious Cabrini-Green project. In September 1993, nine-year-old Anthony Felton was hit by cross fire and killed while playing in front of his home, also in Cabrini-Green. In October 1994, the senseless violence in the Chicago projects hit a new low with the torture and murder of five-year-old Eric Morse, who was hurled out a fourteenth floor window in the Ida B. Well's project by two older boys. His "crime?" He wouldn't help them steal candy.[1]

Hellish conditions in the projects have been thrust into the national consciousness in books such as Alex Kotlowitz's "There are No Children Here: The Story of Two Brothers Growing Up in the Other America" and Sudhir Venkatesh's "American Project," which focus on projects in inner-city Chicago. Lawrence Vale's "From the Puritans to the Projects" documents that even in 1955, there were newspaper accounts of vandalism, delinquency, murder, and assaults on children in the Boston projects.

The terrible situation in the worst projects has given public housing a bad name, but the reality is more complex. As a 1995 government report pointed out, about 3,300 public housing authorities own and operate 13,200 developments, with a total of 1.4 million units. Only 3 percent of housing authorities were classified as "troubled." Yet the eight worst large agencies together accounted for twelve percent of all project units.[2]

The national attention gained by these shocking crimes accelerated an already existing trend to phase out "projects." Beginning with the notorious Pruitt-Igoe project in St. Louis, large-scale high-rise projects have been dynamited. Some of the lost units have been replaced, or are scheduled to be replaced, with smaller "mixed-income" developments under the "Hope VI" program. The Cabrini-Green high rise used by the shooter of Dantrell Davis has already come down, and all of Chicago's high-rise projects will be gone by 2009. Congress stopped funding new construction of large public housing projects twenty years ago, but because of the long life of buildings, many families still live in existing projects. This chapter summarizes the evidence regarding the effects of living in public housing projects, and discusses the many new programs that have grown up as alternatives to the "projects."

An Overview of Public Housing Assistance

Projects represent the most visible "face" of public housing, but they account for less than a quarter of the almost $50 billion that the federal government spends on housing programs for low-income people. Two other major types of programs assist renters.[3] The first type subsidizes the construction or rehabilitation of low-income housing. Under these programs, a builder receives a subsidy in return for agreeing to keep the rent down for a fixed period of time.

No new contracts have been written under these programs since 1983, but because of long lags between the time money is allocated and actual construction, the number of units subsidized by these programs continued to increase for seventeen years after the programs "ended." Many contracts written under these programs will expire by 2006. If the builders do not choose to remain in the program, then they will be able to raise their rents to market rates, and tenants will have to pay more or move out. California alone has 148,540 federally subsidized units, and one in three of the affordable units in Los Angeles stand to become fully privatized in the next few years.[4]

The most rapidly growing federal housing program is the Low Income Housing Tax Credit (LIHTC). The LIHTC offers subsidies to builders in the form of tax credits. To receive a credit, the builder must set aside 20 percent or more of the units to be rent restricted and occupied by very low-income households (households with incomes less than 50 percent of the area median gross income). Alternatively, the builder can set aside 40 percent of the units to be rent restricted and occupied by families whose income is 60 percent or less of the area median gross income. For example, according to the Los Angeles Housing Authority, the median income for a family of four in L.A. is $55,000, and so a four-person family with an income of $27,500 or less would qualify for a rent-restricted apartment in a LIHTC complex meeting the first criteria, while a family earning $33,000 or less would qualify in a complex meeting the second criteria.[5] The rent restrictions must stay in place for thirty years (though earlier projects only had to keep them in place for fifteen years).

Since 1987, about 1.1 million units have been built under LIHTC, and the annual $5 billion in funding for this program produces about 100,000 new units yearly. This program is so popular with developers that only a third of the builders who apply can be funded. This lineup for LIHTC funds suggests that developers are reaping substantial profits from the program, though one advocate for affordable housing construction told me that perhaps private developers did not understand the bureaucratic hurdles that they were in for when they applied.[6] There have also been problems with corruption. The Criminal Investigation Division of the Internal Revenue Service designated the LIHCT program an "emerging issue" for enforcement. According to the IRS's LIHCT newsletter, "[C]ommon fraudulent activities include paying or accepting bribes, falsification of property eligibility, false compliance documentation, falsification of tenant eligibility or altering tenant applications, and inflating occupancy rates."[7]

The third type of assistance available to renters is a "Section 8" voucher. Whether families live in projects or receive vouchers, their rent is capped at 30 percent of their income. Families with vouchers find housing on their own that meets certain conditions (the rent must be less than a specified "fair market rent" and minimum housing standards must be met). The government pays the landlord the difference between the market rent and 30 percent of the family's income.

About 1.3 million families lived in public housing projects in 2002, almost two million received Section 8 vouchers, about 800,000 lived in units subsidized under mostly discontinued builder-subsidy programs, and a further million lived in housing funded under the LIHTC. The numbers cited for federal housing assistance generally include only programs administered by HUD (the Department of Housing and Urban Development) and exclude LIHTC as well as a number of smaller programs administered by the Department of Agriculture. Together these rural programs add up to a considerable expenditure of $9.3 billion (more than is spent on SCHIP or Head Start), though little is known about their effects.[8]

Despite the bad reputation of public housing, huge waiting lists show that demand for both project-based and voucher-based aid continues to far outstrip supply. In New York City, as of March 31, 2004, there were 142,514 families on the waiting list for conventional public housing, 129,551 families on the waiting list for vouchers, and 28,582 families on both waiting lists. In Los Angeles, the average wait for family housing is three years. In Chicago, Boston, and Philadelphia, families can't even get on the waiting list for Section 8 because the lists have been closed—too many families are already waiting. The problem is not confined to large cities—in Shelby County, Alabama, public housing waiting lists for the towns of Columbiana, Calera, and Montevallo have been closed, as have waiting lists in Bloomington, Minnesota.[9]

Public Housing as a Lottery

Waiting lists and closures of waiting lists illustrate the main problem with federal low-income housing programs. Lucky families win the waiting-list lottery and receive a big subsidy. Unlucky families can't even get on a waiting list. In contrast, Medicaid and most nutrition programs are entitlement programs available to all eligible families. Moreover, despite our spending almost as much on housing programs as on medical care for poor women and children, most poor people get no housing assistance. Every housing authority has its own system for ranking eligibles, though most give priority to the elderly, the disabled, families living in substandard housing, or families who have been displaced by government actions. As a result, 43 percent of the households served are above the poverty line; and only 30 percent of renters who are in poverty are served.[10]

One reason that public housing is so unfair, is that it would cost a fortune simply to extend the benefits available under current programs to all eligible families. Under the Housing Act of 1937, a four-person family with an income less than 80 percent of the area's median income is eligible for housing assistance. In Los Angeles County, that would make all four-person households earning $44,100 or less eligible. There are 10 million people in Los Angeles County, and 1.8 million of them are in families below the poverty line who earn far less than $44,100. Much of the entire national budget available for housing programs could be spent in Los Angeles alone!

Housing assistance provides huge subsidies to lucky households. A family without income in Los Angeles could get vouchers worth almost $11,000 for a two-bedroom apartment. If they were fortunate enough to get Section 8 from the City of Santa Monica Housing Authority, this family could receive a voucher worth up to $20,000 for a two-bedroom apartment. Suppose a family had income and was paying over half their income for housing: The housing program would allow this family to reduce their rental payments from 50 to 30 percent of their income; this subsidy would "free up" 20 percent of the family budget to be spent on other things. Specifically, suppose that a poor family of four in Los Angeles earned $18,800 a year and was able to find a modest two-bedroom apartment for $750 per month: Their annual rental payments of $9,000 would eat up 48 percent of their earnings. If they got into the Section 8 program, their rent would be capped at 30 percent of their income. This family would save $4,360 per year, which is greater than the maximum EITC credit of $4,204.

The current allocation of resources makes no sense given that it is the poorest people who are most likely to experience housing problems. The National Low Income Housing Coalition calculated that in 2000 there was no shortage of housing available to households with incomes less than 80 percent of the area median income. In fact, they found that there were 153 housing units available per one hundred renter households. It was only in the group with incomes less than 30 percent of the area median income that a shortage emerged. In this group, only eighty-four units of affordable housing were available for every hundred renter households. Thirty percent of the median income in Los Angeles would be $16,500.[11]

More families could be served with existing resources. Studies have consistently shown that it costs more than a dollar to provide a dollar's worth of housing if that housing is provided in the form of projects. It does not matter whether the projects are built and managed by government or by the private sector. Estimates suggest that it costs at least 35 percent and perhaps as much as 91 percent more to house a family by financing the construction or rehabilitation of housing rather than by giving a Section 8 voucher to the family. A recent government study concluded that current public housing construction programs such as LIHTC and HOPE VI are also more expensive than vouchers, and this study does not even include additional costs to tax payers such as the local property tax abatements that these projects often receive. Moreover, many households with incomes less than 30 percent of the area median income cannot afford to live in LIHTC-sponsored units.[12]

Many housing experts advocate that all project-based assistance be eliminated and changed into vouchers. For example, current public housing project residents could be given vouchers that they could use either to stay in their current locations (though some of the worst housing projects would not even meet Section 8 standards) or move elsewhere. Currently, a family that lives in a project either stays where they are, or walks away from their housing subsidy. So things have to get pretty bad before they will leave. Some families are afraid to try vouchers, fearing that they will be unable to find suitable housing. A policy of "voucherizing" existing projects would allow the system to be switched to vouchers without forcing existing residents to leave. The first Clinton administration suggested this change, as did Robert Dole during his presidential campaign.[13]

The Goals of Public Housing

In order to choose the best housing policy, it is important to be clear about the goal of federal intervention in the housing market. The Housing Act of 1937, which began federal housing programs, was enacted to "remedy the acute shortage of decent, safe, and sanitary dwellings." The Housing Act of 1949 called for the "elimination of substandard and other inadequate housing." Clearly, the primary focus of early legislation was on the quality of the individual housing units themselves.

Inadequate housing is still a concern for many people. Among very low-income renter households with children (defined as households with incomes less than 30 percent of the area median income), 16 percent have housing with "severe or moderate physical problems." That is, their homes may be lacking complete plumbing, have unvented room heaters as primary heating equipment, or have multiple upkeep problems such as water leaks, open cracks, or rats.

Obviously, deficient housing poses a threat to children. Poor sanitation and heating can lead to illness, and diseases such as lead poisoning are directly related to housing conditions. Dangerous conditions in illegally converted garages, laundry rooms, basements, and warehouses are a menace, and the enforcement of housing codes is a continuing headache for local governments. But even among very low-income households, over 80 percent are in housing that is physically adequate.[14]

A second and larger concern is that over 70 percent of these households pay more than 30 percent of their income in rent and utilities. Forty percent pay more than 50 percent of their income for these basics.[15] Families in these circumstances may be forced to cut back on other necessities, even food. In work with Jayanta Bhattacharya and Steven Haider, we found that some poor children ate less in cold snaps—their families were forced to choose whether to "heat or eat."[16] Families paying a high fraction of their income in rent are at increased risk of homelessness, which has devastating impacts on children. Compared to other poor children, homeless children have almost double the rate of school failure and also have higher rates of many health problems.[17]

A third issue that has come to the fore with reports of social breakdown in housing projects is that the neighborhood may also matter. Better neighborhoods are safer and give access to better quality schools, stores, transportation, and jobs. Throwing extremely poor families together in isolated locations leads to downward rather than upward mobility for these families.

The importance of neighborhoods may seem self-evident, but there is actually intense debate among social scientists about whether it is neighborhoods or the child's own family that really matters for children. William Julius Wilson has argued that the increasing concentration of poor black children in neighborhoods with few positive role models has had devastating consequences. Scholars note that jobs have moved away from poor neighborhoods so that "spacial mismatch" makes it difficult for the poor to find work. On the other hand, Susan Mayer and Christopher Jencks point out that the people who move into a given neighborhood differ from those in other neighborhoods before they arrive, and those who leave differ from those who stay. So even if it appears that children from bad neighborhoods do worse than other children, one cannot assume that it is the neighborhood rather than the family that matters. Research on public housing provides some evidence on this point, as discussed later.[18]

Segregation by race and class is the elephant in the room when it comes to discussions of housing policy. Left to itself, the housing market tends to separate the rich and poor—there simply is no low-rent housing to be had in areas such as Bel Air. But the segregated housing market we see today also reflects the effects of past government policies that institutionalized discriminatory practices. In the 1930s, federal regulators in the Home Owners Loan Corporation and the Federal Housing Authority developed the practice of "red-lining" neighborhoods on the basis of race. The best neighborhoods were characterized as "not the home of a single foreigner or Negro." White upper-income gentile neighborhoods received the highest ratings, while the best Jewish neighborhoods could receive only the second highest rating. Neighborhoods with black residents were always given the lowest ratings, which meant that lenders refused to grant mortgage credit in these neighborhoods.[19]

Political "machines" in cities like Chicago strove to maintain racial segregation. The machines opposed efforts by reformers like Robert Taylor, the first black chair of Chicago's Housing Authority. Taylor wished to build public housing units on vacant lots in mostly white neighborhoods throughout the city. His proposal was rejected by the city council. Instead, the city decided that any new public housing would be constructed by tearing down slums in black neighborhoods. Taylor resigned in protest, and it is ironic that one of the worst projects in the city bears his name. When it was completed in 1962, the Robert Taylor Homes became the largest public housing project in the world. Over 4,300 units were packed into twenty-eight sixteen-story high rises in a two-mile stretch isolated from other neighborhoods by the Dan Ryan Expressway.[20]

Beginning in the late 1960s, the federal government reversed course and began legislative efforts to prohibit racial discrimination in lending and housing. Yet racial segregation remains one of the most persistent characteristics of American cities. Segregation is bad for the poor and for minorities since it limits their access to the parks, schools, and shops enjoyed by affluent neighborhoods. It also limits the role models available to poor children. It is also bad for the rich to the extent that it contributes to urban problems such as sprawl and traffic congestion. If all domestic workers in Bel Air must commute two hours from their homes in Riverside County, then this will tie up traffic for the person in the Mercedes as much as for the person in the battered Chevrolet. Segregation is bad for society as a whole if it contributes to a breakdown in social cohesion and the erosion of common values.[21]

A final consideration is that federal housing policy may affect the private provision of affordable housing. Ideally, we want policies that will not discourage private developers from building affordable housing. While there has been little research on this question, some work suggests that when governments build housing units, they do "crowd out" the private sector. One study by Michael Murray found that for every hundred units of subsidized housing built, only seventy-five new units actually came to market. The reason is that twenty-five units of housing that would have been constructed were not built.

A more recent study by Murray distinguishes between conventional public housing and subsidized moderate income housing. This study concludes that conventional public housing has added to the stock of affordable housing (perhaps because private developers are not interested in this segment of the market), but that subsidized moderate income housing has had less impact on the total supply of affordable housing. Research on the effects of smaller projects on property values shows small and inconsistent effects.[22]

The desiderata of federal housing policy are that it be fair in the sense that it treats similar households in a similar way; that it eliminates substandard housing; that it eases the financial burden on families who pay a large share of their incomes in rent; that it improves the neighborhoods available to poor families; that it promotes integration along the lines of race and class; and that it does not reduce the supply or increase the rents in private affordable housing. The perfect policy would meet all these objectives at reasonable cost. Stating the problem this way shows how hard it is. It is difficult for housing policy to meet many goals simultaneously.

Current housing policy obviously fails the fairness test. How close does it come to meeting the other goals? Both project-based aid and vouchers supply housing that meets minimum standards. Both approaches reduce the financial burden on families to 30 percent of income. We have known for more than twenty years that vouchers are a cheaper way to meet these two objectives than building new projects. This means that we could serve more families with the same budget using vouchers. Edgar Olson has calculated that switching all project-based aid to vouchers would allow 900,000 more families to be served.[23]

Given these realities, the fact that project-based aid persists and is growing (recall that the LIHTC is the fastest growing housing program) must reflect the value that legislators place on the other goals of housing policy. The most compelling argument for a policy like LIHTC is that it provides mixed-income developments, which improve the neighborhoods that some poor people live in. Of course, the poor people who are not fortunate enough to live in the LIHTC development may be displaced if rents in their neighborhoods rise as a result of neighborhood improvement, and so even among the poor there will be winners and losers.

The emphasis on mixed-income development reflects a response to the failure of large public housing projects. By concentrating poor families together, large projects create bad neighborhoods. Moreover, many large public housing authorities such as those in Boston and Chicago have records of promoting racial segregation rather than eliminating it. It is possible, though, that the negative effects of project neighborhoods have been exaggerated. The problems of the worst projects may have unjustly tarred the reputations of other projects that do much better. Knowing whether or not the housing provided by a given project is "bad" according to some objective criterion is only part of the equation. If we want to know what effect living in a project has on a child, we also have to know what that child's situation would have been without housing assistance. If, for example, the alternative was to be homeless, or to shift from place to place and school to school, then the stability offered by the project might actually be helpful.

Effects of Housing Policy on Families and Children

In work with Aaron Yelowitz, I found evidence, using a national sample, that even children in projects generally benefit from housing assistance. We find that families with a boy and a girl are more likely to live in public housing than those with two same-sex children, because under public housing rules, they are entitled to larger apartments. Using this finding as a way to separate the effect of living in public housing from the effect of being in a poor family, we find that children in projects were 11 percent less likely to have repeated grades than other similar children, and that they lived in housing that was less crowded. Surprisingly, given the stereotype of large public housing projects, the children in public housing were also less likely to live in buildings with fifty or more units than similar children who were not in public housing.[24]

Brian Jacobs has studied students displaced by demolitions of the most notorious Chicago high-rise projects.[25] Perhaps because of the negative publicity surrounding these buildings, Congress passed a law in 1996 that required local housing authorities to investigate the "viability" of their housing. If the cost of renovating and maintaining a unit was greater than the cost of providing a voucher for twenty years, then the housing authority was required to destroy the unit. As a result of this legislation, 91,000 units, 19,000 of them in Chicago, were slated for demolition.

Jacobs argues that the order in which doomed buildings were destroyed was determined by outside events and was approximately random. For example, in January 1999, the pipes froze in some buildings in the Robert Taylor Homes, which meant that those buildings were demolished before others in the same complex. By comparing children who stayed in buildings scheduled to be demolished to others who had already been displaced by demolitions, he obtains a measure of the effect of living in high-rise public housing.

The high rises in Jacob's study are among the worst public-housing projects in the country. So it is surprising that he finds that giving vouchers to the residents and allowing them to relocate had very little effect on their children's educations. Displaced families were much less likely to live in public housing after building closures, but most children in these families stayed in similar neighborhoods, attended similar schools, and experienced similar educational outcomes as those who stayed in the most notorious high rises.

The fact that project residents tend to stay in poor neighborhoods when they are offered vouchers has been found in many other studies. For example, a comprehensive review of the Experimental Housing Allowance Program (which is discussed later) found that vouchers (housing allowances) had little effect on racial or economic segregation.[26] This may reflect constraints on poor households. Susan Popkin and Mary Cunningham show that it can be hard to lease an apartment using a Section 8 voucher. It is costly to search for an apartment in a new neighborhood, especially if a family must rely on public transportation. The family may have difficulty scraping together a security deposit or passing credit checks.

Large families find it especially difficult to find apartments, and there is anecdotal evidence of substantial bias against holders of Section 8 certificates by landlords. It is possible that the landlords discriminate against people with these vouchers. Alternatively, the bias against people with Section 8 vouchers might indicate that landlords don't like dealing with the local public housing authority. One case study of fifty-six single mothers in Massachusetts found that after waiting an average of two years for their vouchers, twenty-four women returned them unused. These women were unable to find housing that met Section 8 requirements within the allotted time.[27]

There may be many barriers that prevent families from moving to other neighborhoods, but it is also possible that many low-income families choose to live in neighborhoods they are familiar with because they have ties to family and friends. The most exhaustive examination of the effects of giving vouchers to project residents is an ongoing experiment called "Moving to Opportunity" (MTO).

MTO was inspired by the Gautreaux program in Chicago. This program allowed residents of some black public housing projects to move to white suburbs. Gautreaux was the result of a discrimination lawsuit filed against the Chicago Housing Authority (CHA) and HUD in 1966 on behalf of Chicago public housing residents. The suit alleged that the CHA had conspired to segregate black and white residents. The Chicago Housing Authority established the Gautreaux program as part of a consent decree in 1976.

Under Gautreaux, project households who paid their rent on time and had adequate housekeeping abilities could apply for Section 8 housing vouchers and move to private apartments. Some apartments were in the inner city, while others were in predominantly white suburbs. Applicants were offered whatever apartment happened to be available when their name came to the top of the list. Most applicants accepted the apartment that they were offered because otherwise, they would have dropped back to the bottom of the waiting list.

In a series of studies of this program James Rosenbaum argues that this means that the Gautreaux families were approximately randomly assigned to different kinds of neighborhoods. If this is true, then we can gauge the effects of neighborhoods simply by comparing the outcomes of children who moved to different places. That is, Gautreaux provides a naturally occurring experiment similar to a drug trial in which "treatments" get the new drug and the "controls" get a sugar pill.

Rosenbaum found that children who had moved to the suburbs (the treatments) attended better schools than those who stayed in the inner city (the controls). When they were interviewed seven years later, children who had moved to the suburbs were 15 percent less likely to have dropped out, 16 percent more likely to be in a college-track program, and 34 percent more likely to be employed than those who had moved to apartments in the inner city. In addition, the children's mothers were 25 percent more likely to have a job.

There was some controversy about the validity of these results, since 41 percent of the original study children could not be found. To continue the analogy of the drug trial, if we started with one hundred people and fifty got the new drug while fifty got the placebo, we would be seriously disturbed if we could find only fifty-nine people at the end of the study. We would ask what had happened to the others? Perhaps they died or dropped out due to serious side effects? We would want to know. In the Gautreaux case, it is possible that the children who dropped out of the study also dropped out of school. Simply ignoring these children could give a very misleading picture of the impact of the move to the suburbs on all of the "treated" children.[28]

MTO is a large-scale social experiment that is being conducted in Chicago, New York, Los Angeles, Boston, and Baltimore. Between 1994 and 1998, volunteers from public housing projects were assigned by lottery to one of three groups. The first group received a voucher that could be used to rent housing only in a low-poverty area (a Census tract with a poverty rate less than 10 percent). This group also received help locating a suitable apartment. I will call this the MTO group. The second group received a normal Section 8 voucher that they could use to rent an apartment in any neighborhood. The third group was the control and received no vouchers or assistance, although they continued to remain eligible for their project apartment.

Families in the first group did move to lower-poverty neighborhoods. At the beginning of the experiment, 94 percent of the MTO group lived in neighborhoods with poverty rates of 36 percent or more. When families were followed up in 2002, 60 percent of experimentals were in Census tracts with poverty rates of 20 percent or less compared to 30 percent of the Section 8 group and 17 percent of control families. The new neighborhoods of the MTO families were also significantly safer than their old neighborhoods.

Contrary to expectations, the move to new neighborhoods had positive effects on girls but had either no effect, or negative effects, on boys. Girls in the MTO group were more likely than controls to graduate from high school and were much less likely to suffer from anxiety. Girls in the regular Section 8 group also experienced improvements in mental health relative to the controls. Finally, girls in the MTO and Section 8 groups were much less likely to have ever been arrested than controls.

In contrast, boys in the experimental group were 13 percent more likely than controls to have ever been arrested. This increase was due largely to increases in property crimes. These boys also report more risky behaviors such as drug and alcohol use. Also, boys in the MTO and voucher groups were more likely to suffer injuries. These differences between boys and girls are apparent even within families.

MTO researchers are so far at a loss to explain these gender differences. It is possible that boys have a harder time than girls socializing with others in their new neighborhoods and react by becoming disaffected and delinquent. Or perhaps these predominantly black boys faced more discrimination in their new neighborhoods than black girls and responded accordingly. In any case, the results of MTO suggest that moving children from projects to wealthier neighborhoods is not a panacea.[29]

It remains to be seen how the long-term outcomes of the MTO children will differ from controls. Philip Oreopoulos has conducted one of the few rigorous studies to have addressed the long-run consequences of living in a poor neighborhood. Oreopoulos uses data from Canadian income tax records to examine the earnings of adults who lived in public housing projects in Toronto as children. There are large differences between projects in Toronto, both in terms of the density of the projects, and in terms of the poverty of the neighborhoods. As in the Gautraux project, the type of project a family lives in is approximately randomly assigned because the family is offered whatever happens to be available when they get to the top of the waiting list. Oreopoulos finds that once he controls for the characteristics of the family, the neighborhood has no effect on future earnings or the likelihood that someone works. These results are consistent with what would expect on the basis of the MTO evaluations.[30]

Should We Use Vouchers Instead of Projects?

The main argument for preferring project-based programs such as LIHTC to vouchers is that mixed-income developments enable some poor people to move to better neighborhoods. Against this, we must set the higher costs of project-based aid and the unfairness of helping some families while leaving others behind. Moreover, the fact that the project-based aid costs more means that fewer families can be helped with any given budget. The evidence suggests that the importance of moving poor people to mixed-income neighborhoods has been exaggerated. If this is true, then the major argument in favor of project-based housing aid may be invalid.

A number of other arguments are often advanced against voucher programs. First, some families have difficulty using vouchers and return them unused—but the fact that some vouchers are returned does not mean that any are wasted. The number of families that are allowed to search at any point in time is greater than the number of vouchers. For example, if only 50 percent of searchers were expected to be successful in a given search period, a housing authority could make sure that all of the vouchers were used by authorizing twice as many people to search as they had vouchers for. This is the same principal as airlines use when they overbook flights. Unlike the airlines, which sometimes turn passengers away, housing authorities have a reserve fund to ensure that everyone who successfully finds an apartment is able to rent it.

The system works so well that at any point in time over 90 percent of the available vouchers are being used. Even though only 56 percent of families given permission to search for a Section 8 apartment in Los Angeles find suitable housing, Los Angeles has been able to increase its voucher-utilization rate from 84 to 96 percent. The L.A. housing authority achieved this by conducting outreach to property owners and streamlining its administrative procedures. In other housing markets, much higher fractions of families given permission to search are able to find housing.[31]

Similarly, low vacancy rates in a particular housing market don't mean that voucher recipients won't be able to find housing. Many voucher recipients are able to use their vouchers to stay in their existing apartments. Stephen Kennedy and Meryl Finkel examined data from thirty-three housing authorities and found that outside New York City (which they examined separately) 30 percent of voucher recipients stayed in the apartments they were in. Forty-one percent of these apartments already met Section 8 standards and the rest were repaired to meet the standards. Of the 70 percent of recipients who moved to new apartments, about half moved into apartments that were upgraded to meet Section 8 standards. In New York City, which has a very tight housing market, only 31 percent of the apartments that Section 8 recipients lived in had to be repaired to meet program standards.[32]

These results show that greater availability of Section 8 vouchers would encourage landlords to repair existing housing. This conclusion is supported by evidence from the Experimental Housing Allowance Program (EHAP). Part of this experiment involved running a voucher program for ten years in South Bend, Indiana, and Green Bay, Wisconsin. Unlike Section 8 vouchers, the EHAP vouchers were available to all low-income households in the counties. Landlords were motivated to fix their apartments to qualify for EHAP vouchers because given that all the low-income households now had vouchers, EHAP was the only game in town. Also, you would expect that the fact that the tenants had vouchers would allow landlords to charge somewhat higher rents, which would again give them a motivation for participating in the program. Over the first five years of the experiment, 11,000 homes were repaired to meet program standards. Helen Cutts and Edgar Olsen point out that this program produced a greater increase in the supply of affordable housing in these areas than all of the federal government's project-based programs had ever produced—and the average cost was only $3,000 per unit in current dollars.[33]

The potential increase in rents at the bottom of the market is a drawback of a large voucher program like EHAP. If poor people with a voucher are willing to pay more for apartments than they would without a voucher, rents will rise. If rents go up enough, then landlords rather than poor people will gain. Moreover, if rents rise, then a voucher program that undertook to pay the whole difference between market rents and 30 percent of the renter's income would become more expensive. But if the supply of low-rent apartments also increases in response to the voucher program, then the effects on rents will be mitigated. So whether a large-scale voucher program would drive up rents and by how much is an empirical question that cannot be answered through theorizing about the problem.

The Experimental Housing Allowance Program looked at this question and found that voucher programs had little effect on market rents. The markets involved in this program all had vacancy rates of around 7 percent. It is possible that in extremely tight housing markets with lower vacancy rates, rents would rise. In this case, the cost of providing housing through vouchers would become more comparable to the cost of new construction. In most housing markets, however, vouchers clearly dominate.[34]

There are several different ways in which a voucher program could be more strongly targeted to low-income families. In fact, by switching to an all-voucher policy we could create an entitlement program that served all of the poorest families at the same cost as current housing policies. Dirk Early and Edgar Olsen argue that such a policy would largely eliminate homelessness among families.[35] Still, Christopher Jencks's path-breaking study of homelessness found that the majority of the 300,000 to 600,000 homeless were single men with substance abuse problems or mental illness, not families. Jencks argues that even this population could benefit from housing voucher programs, but that other policies, such as changing zoning to allow single-room occupancy dwellings and restoring psychiatric hospital beds for the hard-core mentally ill, are necessary to make a real dent in homelessness. Other analysts, such as Martha Burt and Laudan Aron distinguish between people experiencing short-term crises (which might be solved by preventive measures such as emergency financial aid) and the chronically homeless. For the latter, they advocate transitional housing with supportive services. For both groups, they argue that programs (including rental assistance through vouchers) that make housing more affordable are necessary.[36]

Some of these ideas are being implemented. Homelessness skyrocketed in New York City as flop-houses were converted to luxury apartments in the 1970s and early 1980s. By 1985, 100,000 cheap single-occupancy rooms had been lost. In 1988, the city created a loan program to assist nonprofit sponsors who wanted to renovate or construct single-room occupancy units (SROs) and other housing for the homeless. These sponsors often provide drug, alcohol, and mental health counseling in the same building. These programs have been credited with reducing homelessness, and they are being imitated by other cities. One study found that after five years, 88 percent of formerly homeless people with mental health problems who had been helped by the "Pathways to Housing" program remained housed. In contrast, only 47 percent of homeless people who had been helped through the city's traditional residential treatment system were off the streets. This program subsidizes up to 70 percent of the cost of housing through Section 8 and local, state, and federal grants.[37]

San Franciso used to give homeless people $410 per month. Mayor Gavin Newsom says, "No other major city in America hands out as much cash, which is why all the Bay Area homeless come here—San Mateo gives fifty-eight dollars, Alameda twenty-five, and Chicago gives no dollars—but all we're doing is reinforcing failure. . . . Check day is when drug dealers come to town, emergency rooms are overwhelmed, there's a precipitous drop in shelter use. It's a vicious cycle of despair—a hundred and sixty-nine homeless people died in this city last year." Newsom's answer has been the "Care not Cash" program, which has cut the cash to between $59 and $97 per month and is aggressively building SROs. Nearly 940 units were to have been built or renovated by the end of 2004.[38]

Providing housing for poor families is clearly different than providing housing for homeless single adults with substance abuse or mental health problems. One way to target existing funds to low-income families is to lower the income cutoffs for eligibility. Congress has already moved in this direction. Since 1998, 75 percent of new vouchers have been directed to families with incomes less than 30 percent of the area median income, as long as any of these families are on the waiting list. For example, in Los Angeles new vouchers to four-person families go mainly to people with incomes less than $16,538, although families with incomes less than $44,100 remain technically eligible.

A second option would be to reduce the size of the subsidy available to each family. The maximum amount that a family with no income can receive is called the payment standard. The voucher pays the difference between 30 percent of the family's income and the payment standard. In Los Angeles, the payment standard for a two-bedroom apartment is $905. Lowering the payment standard would reduce the number of higher-income families eligible to participate in the program. For example, if the payment standard was $600 per month, then any family earning more than $24,000 would be ineligible for housing assistance. The reason is that $7,200 (twelve times $600) is already less than 30 percent of their income.

An objection to lowering the payment standard is that the poorest families might not be able to rent anything with a subsidy of only $600 per month. Housing authorities can also be expected to oppose this measure strongly because lower subsidies would make it harder for families successfully to find apartments. This in turn, would raise the administrative costs of the program. But research suggests that in most housing markets the payment standards are higher than the minimum required to rent an apartment meeting Section 8 standards. Amy Cutts and Edgar Olsen calculate that the payment standard exceeded the minimum subsidy by a median of 68 percent in 2001. So payment standards could be lowered by a considerable amount, and the poorest families would still be able to find units meeting Section 8 standards.[39]

A third way to target the program on the poorest would be to increase the fraction of their income that families must pay above 30 percent. A family with no income won't care whether they are charged 30 or 40 percent of their nonexistent income, but a family making more money will. If many poor families are currently paying more than half of their incomes for rent, then fixing the rent share at 40 percent of their incomes and serving more families would be fairer than the current policy of reducing some family's rent burdens to 30 percent while leaving others unassisted. None of these measures to reduce the size of housing benefits is attractive.

They make sense only in the context of a broader policy that would make housing benefits an entitlement for all poor families.

Summary

Current housing policy does not meet its goals. The system has the flavor of a lottery in which a few lucky families "win big," while most are left out in the cold. Nevertheless, the system could be greatly improved by building on some of its existing elements, in particular, the housing voucher program. A rational housing policy would begin by eliminating construction subsidy programs and projects in favor of voucher programs that served *everyone* below a given income level. Future policymakers could then argue about whether this target income level should be moved up or down. The current policy of providing big subsidies to some families while others cannot even get on waiting lists is indefensible.

More families could be served with the same budget if all spending were switched from construction programs to voucher programs. Such a switch is likely to have few negative consequences. Still, the emphasis on serving more families with the same budget raises the question of whether we should also be spending more money on housing for the poor in total. The obvious comparison is to the amount that we spend on housing for those who are better off.

Tax deductions for mortgage interest, property taxes, capital gains, and investments in housing are expected to total $120 billion per year between 2002 and 2007. The more expensive your house is, the higher your tax deduction, so these benefits go mainly to those who are better off. People do not think about these "tax expenditures" in the same way that they think about government spending, but from the point of view of the federal budget, they are the same. Income taxes that are not collected cannot be spent on other programs such as national defense or highways. Given the large tax expenditures on home owners, the expenditures on housing for the poor are extremely modest.[40]

Looking backwards offers a second way to get some perspective on these numbers. In 1978 the annual appropriation for HUD's housing programs was $75 billion in current dollars. Spending fell sharply under the first Reagan administration, to $16 billion by 1983. The number of new families helped each year also dropped precipitously. Housing expenditures for the poor have been highly variable and even large increases would be well within the spending we have allocated to these programs in the past.[41] Hence there is a case to be made both for a radical restructuring of existing programs and for increases in expenditures on these programs.

Chapter 5

Who's Minding the Kids?

Anne Adkisson left welfare in 2001 to take an $8.66 per hour job as an aide in a child-care center. With state subsidies, she could afford to send her two-year-old to a child-care center and enroll her nine-year-old in an after-school program. In 2003, state cutbacks eliminated her child-care subsidy. Unable to pay $125 per week for child care, she began leaving the toddler with relatives and leaving work early to pick up the nine-year-old from school. She laments that her daughter is "missing out" on what she would learn at the center. Shorter hours are also making it more difficult for her to get ahead.[1] This anecdote illustrates the dual role of child care in the safety net. Without safe, reliable, enriching child care, both children and parents often lose.

The debate about government funding of child care is emotional and complex. Some argue that children should stay home with a parent, at least for their earliest years. A huge body of literature on the effects of maternal employment suggests that a mother's employment in the first year of life may have small harmful effects on children. Other recent studies find that children who are in child care for many hours a day experience increases in stress and are more likely to have behavior problems down the road. On the other hand, many studies have reported that children who attended preschool do better in school, though this may be partly because middle-class children are more likely to attend than poor children.[2]

Among older children, the "latch key" phenomena is worrying. In 1999, 10.5% of five- to fourteen-year-old children of employed mothers were unsupervised for part of the day. The fraction of children who are unsupervised rises sharply with age. Only 8.1 percent of nine year olds are left unsupervised compared to 44.9 percent of fourteen year olds. Children left to their own devices are at increased risk of truancy, poor grades, and risky behaviors of all sorts. Juvenile crime rates triple between 3 and 6 p.m., when children are most likely to be left unattended. Children are also most likely to be victims of violent crimes committed by people outside their families in these after-school hours. Clearly, lack of supervision is a serious problem, at least for some children.[3]

Whatever the pros and cons of parental vs. nonparental care, many children have parents who must work to support them. Other parents face a difficult choice between extra income and the family time that must be sacrificed to earn it. The research to date has not offered much guidance to parents about this trade-off. Saying that children would be better off in maternal care, holding income constant, does not describe the reality most families face. In 2000, 65.3% of single women with children under six were in the work force. The majority of infants are placed in some sort of nonmaternal care by four months of age. Even mothers who do not work use child care. A third of their infants to four-year-old children are in nonparental care for an average of more than twenty hours per week. This chapter discusses the federal government's growing involvement in the market for child care.

The Government and Child Care—An Overview

The government is a major player in the child-care market, covering a third of the costs of child care for children less than six. So it makes sense to ask how child-care policy affects vulnerable children and their families.[4] The government intervenes in the market for child care in four major ways: through tax credits, subsidies, regulation, and by directly funding care.

One of the oldest government child care "programs" is the Dependent Care Tax Credit (DCTC), which cost the government $2.8 billion in forgone tax revenues in 2001. While this credit is often touted as an important benefit for working families, it does not benefit the poor. The maximum expense that any family with two children can claim is $6,000. A family with $6,000 in expenses and an income less than $15,000 would be eligible to claim the maximum possible credit of $2,000. But in practice, virtually no one can claim the maximum credit because families with incomes below $15,000 cannot afford to spend $6,000 on child care. More importantly, these low-income families are unlikely to owe any taxes, and so they cannot take the credit. Unlike the Earned Income Tax Credit, the DCTC is not "refundable." Beginning in 1989, families have had to report the taxpayer identification number of the care provider to claim the credit. This provision caused the number of DCTC claims filed to drop by a third from 9 million in 1988 to 6 million in 1989. Since poor families are more likely to rely on care by relatives and other informal, unregulated, and unreported arrangements, they were disproportionately impacted by this change.[5]

Poor families spend a much higher fraction of their incomes on child-care expenses than richer ones—29 compared to 7 percent. This is hardly surprising, given that the average annual child-care tuition is over $3,300 per child. Recognizing that these families needed help, the welfare reform act of 1996 (PRWPRA) consolidated several existing child-care subsidy programs. There is now a single block grant from the federal government to the states, called the Child Care and Development Fund (CCDF). Poor families are much more likely to rely on these subsidies than on tax credits.

States have also been allowed to use money from their TANF and Social Security Block Grant (SSBG) programs to pay for child care. As a result, child-care subsidies grew rapidly after 1996 as welfare rolls declined. In fact, most of the increase in state spending on child care has been financed by using funds originally earmarked for other programs like TANF rather than by new monies from the federal government. In 2002, $3.7 billion in TANF funds and $200 million in SSBG funds were used for child-care programs, compared to the $3.9 billion in federal funds that were directly authorized for the child care block grant.[6]

The fact that child care money has been given to states in the form of a block grant may seem arcane but has important consequences. First, rules governing the subsidies are set at the state level and vary greatly from state to state. In 2002, the monthly income cutoff for child-care subsidies varied from $3,501 in Minnesota to $1,482 in Missouri. Some states charge fees to poor families, while others do not. States that charge fees set them many different ways, including charging flat rates, percent of cost, and percent of income. States are supposed to set the child-care subsidy rate high enough that most providers would be willing to accept a child eligible for the state subsidy. Many states use out-of-date market rate surveys, however, to get around this requirement, or they simply ignore it.[7]

A second consequence of the block-grant format is that recent state budget crises are having an impact on child care subsidy programs. Between 2001 and 2004, most states lowered their income cutoffs—for example, Minnesota reduced the cutoff to $2,225 from $3,501 per month. Almost half the states now have long waiting lists for child-care subsidies. As of early 2004, 280,000 children were on waiting lists in California, 46,000 were waiting in Florida, and 26,000 were waiting in Texas, despite the higher eligibility requirements. Many states have also increased their fees—for example, in Michigan, a family's monthly fee rose by $122 between 2001 and 2004.[8] These cutbacks have intensified controversy about whether the families who most need the subsidies are actually getting them. A third consequence of the block grant approach is that it is hard to tell exactly who is benefiting from these federal funds. Every state maintains its own database. Available estimates of the fraction of eligible children served vary wildly. In 2000 the federal government issued a news release saying that only 12 percent of the children eligible for child-care subsidies were receiving them. This report counted all children under thirteen in families with a working parent and an income less than 85 percent of the state median income as eligible. In 2002 the same government agency reported that 59 percent of needy preschool children were receiving services, but this time the needy were defined as children in poor families whose heads worked at least twenty hours per week.[9]

These diverging numbers reflect value judgments about who deserves help and who needs care as much as they reflect cold hard facts. An alternative approach to determining need is to survey potential recipients. For example, a survey of welfare mothers in northern California found that only 37 to 44 percent of women using child care received a subsidy, even though all of these mothers were eligible.[10] A study of administrative data from Illinois, Maryland, and Masschusetts matched state unemployment insurance records (which record earnings) to data on child-care subsidies. It found that take-up rates among eligible mothers were never greater than 35 percent.[11] In their survey, Anne Witte and Magaly Queralt distinguish between states that guarantee subsidies to eligible families (where about 40 percent of eligibles are served) and those that do not offer such guarantees (where the numbers served are much lower).[12]

It is not completely clear why so many eligible mothers are not served. While some women may not want care, one study reported that the biggest reason why eligible women did not use subsidies is that they did not know about them.[13] Women who are eligible and find out about the programs still run into many barriers. Many states have frozen intakes and put applicants on waiting lists (as of March 2000, seventeen states had done so) because they did not have enough funds to serve all eligible applicants. In these cases, TANF families usually receive priority over other poor families. Administrative barriers may also be daunting—in many states, parents with subsidies must report all changes in income, work status, work schedules, and provider (whether or not they impact the subsidy the person is entitled to). These reporting requirements may force parents repeatedly to take time off work, defeating the point of the subsidy. One study in five states found that the average length of subsidy receipt was only three to seven months, suggesting that families have a hard time complying with the requirements for maintaining eligibility.[14]

It is not surprising, then, to find that child-care subsidies have modest effects on the employment of single mothers. For example, one study compared mothers on a waiting list for child care to those who had already obtained subsidies and found that the subsidies increased the probability of employment by about 8 percent. A second study looked at the implicit subsidy provided by free public kindergartens. The study focused on a comparison of families in which the youngest child had just missed the age cutoff for kindergarten, and families whose youngest child was just old enough to go. This study found that among single mothers of five-year-olds, those whose youngest was eligible for kindergarten were about 5 percent more likely to be employed. The Chapin Hall study discussed earlier also addressed these issues, and once again showed that subsidies increase maternal employment modestly. As we have seen in previous chapters, we would not expect these changes in maternal employment to have a large impact on children's outcomes.[15] Recent work by Erdal Tekin suggests that child-care subsidies help women to find employment during traditional working hours, rather than night shifts and other nonstandard hours. The effect of these more subtle types of changes in mother's work are not known.[16]

Subsidy programs also promote the use of paid care, by making it cheaper. If paid care was of higher quality than the free care provided by friends and relatives, then this might be good for children. The Achilles' heel of efforts to ensure quality is that they rely on the states' existing regulatory apparatus to monitor quality, and there is much evidence that many states are doing a bad job.

State Regulation of Child Care

Every state has regulations governing pupil-teacher ratios, teacher training, and health and safety. Effective regulation should eliminate threats to health and safety—and by assuring parents of a minimal level of quality, it could encourage people to use regulated child care. But it is possible that the existence of regulation creates a false sense of security in parents given that regulations set minimum standards and that even these standards often go unenforced.[17]

Regulations vary a great deal from state to state. In child-care centers, Kansas, Maryland and Massachusetts require one staff member for every three infants, while eight other states allow one care giver to look after six infants. For four-year-old children, the child-staff ratio in centers varies from ten-to-one to twenty-to-one. Thirty-two states don't require any child-care experience or special training of teachers in day-care centers. Others require specific training in early childhood education. The frequency of state inspections also varies from once every two years to three or four times a year.

Regulations are typically much weaker for day-care services operated out of family homes than for centers, and the smallest providers are often legally exempt from any regulation at all. In some states, such as Illinois, Indiana, and in the District of Columbia, over half of the children served by CCDF subsidy money use providers who are exempt from regulation. In Illinois, providers who want to receive a subsidy only have to fill in a form promising that their home is safe, that they will care for no more than three unrelated children, and that they have no history of child abuse or neglect. No attempt is made to verify these claims. In some poor neighborhoods, over 90 percent of the subsidized child care is unlicensed.[18]

Overstretched state agencies often seem unable to enforce even the minimal regulations that exist. In 1999, Louisville's *Courier-Journal* conducted an investigation of records from annual state inspections of day-care records and found that 73 percent of the centers that they examined had violated state regulations at least once in the past two years, and many had multiple violations. The centers were most commonly cited for being understaffed or having undertrained and inattentive staff. One center was cited for having only one teacher for seventeen children—eleven more than are permitted by Kentucky's regulations. The report indicated that when staff left eight toddlers alone in a room, one crawled onto a table, while two others nearly pulled a phone off a shelf onto their heads. Centers were frequently cited for filthy bathrooms, dirty kitchens, and spoiled food. A center in Pennsylvania that had been licensed to serve twenty-eight children recently closed after the owner's own relatives reported unsafe conditions to the state. The center had exposed electrical wires, lacked smoke alarms, and had emergency exits that were nailed shut. The owner's sister said, "We were afraid for the children's safety. I have four children and I'd never allow any of my children to be in here."[19]

Following an incident in which an unattended seven-month-old suffocated under a pile of toys, New York-WABC TV launched an undercover investigation of the regulation of child-care centers and family homes in New York City. Their investigator went to the health department posing as a mom interested in a day care that was operating illegally because its license had been revoked. She was not given any information about the center's numerous safety and health violations, or about the revocation of its license. The report points out that at the same time, the health department website posted detailed information about health violations at all of the city's restaurants, and laments "It is too bad the day care isn't a restaurant."[20]

The Importance of Child-Care Quality

The comparison of child-care centers to restaurants highlights the limitations of regulation. While inspectors can ensure that restaurants are clean, they cannot ensure that the food is good. Similarly, child care regulators do not even attempt to measure more subtle measures of quality. In addition to safe, sanitary conditions, children need

> caregivers [who] encourage children to be actively engaged in a variety of activities; have frequent, positive interactions with children that include smiling, touching, holding, and speaking at children's eye level; promptly respond to children's ques-

tions or requests; and encourage children to talk about their experience, feelings, and ideas. Caregivers in high-quality settings also listen attentively, ask open-ended questions and extend children's actions and verbalizations with more complex ideas or materials, interact with children individually and in small groups instead of exclusively with the group as a whole, use positive guidance techniques, and encourage appropriate independence.[21]

There are no national data on these aspects of child-care quality, but two large-scale studies have tried to measure it using scales that have been developed for this purpose. Both studies conclude that the average center is about halfway between "minimal" and "good" quality, a level that one study dubbed "mediocre." Infant-toddler rooms generally have the worst ratings, and nonprofit centers get higher ratings than for profits. One study reported that 10 percent of the child-care centers that they examined were of such poor quality that they threatened children's health and safety. Informally, one leading researcher on child-care quality confided that child care at the lowest level of the quality rankings is so bad that it "makes your skin crawl."[22]

State regulation may eventually weed out persistently substandard centers. By their nature, however, regulations impose minimum standards rather than trying to define optimal standards of care. Hence, even centers that meet all state standards may still be of low quality. Moreover, there seems to be a weak relationship between quality defined using the things measured by state standards, and quality defined in terms of things like a warm and stimulating environment.[23]

If states did try to define and enforce a high standard of quality in child-care centers and licensed family homes, they would run into a new problem. Complying with regulations—by, for example, increasing staff and staff training—is costly. These costs will be passed on in the form of higher fees. Higher fees, in turn, drive parents out of high-quality, regulated care and into unregulated care. Since poor parents are likely to be most sensitive to price, they are most likely to be driven out of the regulated child-care market. Hence, stricter regulation will benefit poor parents only if steps are taken to ensure that they retain access to the high-quality care that such regulation could bring.[24]

This discussion raises an obvious question: Where are the parents? How is it possible that people are paying money for care of such low quality that it endangers their children? What sort of parent would send her child to a day-care center that had bare electrical wires dangling and emergency exits that were nailed shut? The most charitable explanation is that many parents just aren't very good at judging quality. Most parents find out about child-care providers by asking friends and relatives. If these friends and relatives don't know about good-quality child care in the area, then the parent will not either. When asked about specific aspects of their child's care, parents give systematically higher ratings than trained observers. Parents also tend to place great weight on things that are objectively irrelevant to the quality of care (such as the cleanliness of the waiting area), while ignoring other indicators (such as how many books are available to the children).[25]

One reaction to these arguments is to reject the experts' measures of child-care quality. Perhaps the experts are just out of touch with what people value, and with what is good for children. Parents typically say, however, that they value the same things as the experts, though they also value things like a convenient location and economical cost. Moreover, parents who have more education and income rate their child-care settings in a way that is more similar to a trained observer. These arguments suggest that parents' lack of information about the quality of care constitutes an important rationale for government intervention in the child care market—it is impossible for the private market to operate efficiently if people cannot properly verify the quality of services that they purchase.

As a new parent, the prospect of finding a care giver for my babies scared me to death. As my children have grown, I have used different child-care settings and observed that even wealthy, well-educated parents cannot always tell a good child-care setting from a bad one. For example, if you point out that staff are not washing their hands after helping children with toileting, parents will agree that this is a problem, but they will not necessarily notice the problem in the first place. More seriously, these same parents may privately note that a teacher seems punitive, inattentive, or downright incompetent, but often do not have enough confidence in their own judgment of child-care quality to act. If these wealthy and well-educated parents are unable to rectify problems with their child's care, then it should not be surprising that parents who command fewer resources and have few good alternative sources of care often fail to do so as well.

The Benefits of Quality Care

Aside from obvious threats to the health and safety of children that are posed by low-quality care, we should care about the quality of the child care available to poor children because it is precisely these children who have the most to gain from high-quality care. Providing good-quality care to poor children is one of the most effective ways of breaking the intergenerational cycle of poverty. Hence, children like Anne Adkisson's toddler really are missing out on something important when they are excluded from participation in a high-quality child-care setting.

Many studies attempt to measure the "effect" of child care quality by comparing the outcomes of children who were in good-quality care to the outcomes of children who were not. An obvious problem with this strategy is that one would expect children in good-quality care to have all sorts of other advantages over other children, especially given the high cost of such care. One of the more compelling studies of the issue is being conducted by the government's National Institutes of Child Health and Human Development. The Study of Early Child Care has followed a large group of children from their birth in 1991 up to the present. A study of these children at age four-and-a-half implied that children in care of medium quality had slightly higher test scores than children in poor-quality care, where quality was measured using scales that take account of the more subtle aspects of quality described earlier. This study took many differences in family background into account, and also looked at gains in test scores between ages two and four-and-a-half.[26] It is concerned with the average effect of child-care quality on the average child; but studies of interventions for poor children show much larger effects.

The most convincing evidence of the positive role that child care can play comes from experiments in which disadvantaged children were randomly assigned to a treatment group that got high-quality care, and a control group that did not. Much of the early literature evaluating these interventions was obsessed with changing IQ scores. Unfortunately, while it is relatively easy to create short-term gains in IQ test scores, it is hard to generate long-term effects. Yet there is growing recognition that IQ isn't everything. A recent National Research Council report on early childhood education divides skill development into three parts: cognitive skills, school readiness, and social and emotional development. It will not surprise parents to learn that the ability to sit still, pay attention, and follow direction is just as important to success in the early school years as the ability to recite the ABCs. This means that early intervention could have long-lasting effects on schooling attainment and other outcomes, even if it did not increase IQ. This is precisely what the best studies have found.[27]

Three studies of "model" early intervention child-care programs stand out because they randomly assigned children to treatment and control group, had low dropout rates, and followed children at least into middle school.[28] The three studies are the Carolina Abecedarian Project, the Perry Preschool Project, and the Milwaukee Project. (A fourth, the Infant Health and Development Project also used a randomized design and had few dropouts, but followed children only to age eight. A long-term followup is currently in the field.) Of these, only the Milwaukee Project found any long-term effect on IQ, but the Carolina Abecedarian and Perry Preschool Projects both found positive effects on schooling.

The Carolina Abecedarian Project involved fifty-seven treatments and fifty-four controls from poor families. Children in the treatment group went to a very high-quality child care for eight hours per day, five days a week, fifty weeks per year, from birth to age five. Children in the control group got no special services. In the Abcedarian center, the teacher-pupil ratio ranged from 1:3 to 1:6, depending on the child's age, and the teachers were highly trained, especially in language development. At age fifteen, the Abecedarian children had higher scores on achievement tests (especially reading) and reductions in the incidence of grade retention and special education. Failing grades and being placed in the special education "track" are important indicators because they predict which children are at risk of high school dropout. At age twenty-one, the children who had gone to the child-care centers still had higher average tests scores and were twice as likely as the controls to still be in school or to have ever attended a four-year college. A recent cost-benefit analysis of the data through age twenty-one found that each dollar spent on Abecedarian saved tax payers four dollars. By focusing only on cost savings, this calculation does not even include the value of higher achievement to the individual children and society.[29]

The Perry Preschool Project followed fifty-eight treatment children and sixty-five controls from poor inner-city families. Treatment children went to a half-day preschool every weekday and had weekly ninety-minute home visits for eight months of the year, for two years. Teacher/student ratios were one to six, and all of the teachers had Master's degrees and training in child development. As of age twenty-seven, the intervention had positive effects on achievement test scores, grades, high school graduation rates, and earnings, as well as negative effects on crime and welfare use. Each dollar spent on Perry Preschool saved up to seven dollars in social costs.[30]

The Head Start Program

No one questions that these interventions had dramatic effects. Yet they involved very few children and intensive high-quality programs. Debate rages about whether it is feasible to give all poor children the same opportunity these children received, and if not, whether lesser interventions will still have a positive impact? The best evidence on this question is provided by evaluations of the federal Head Start program. Head Start is a preschool program for disadvantaged three-, four-, and five-year-olds which currently serves about 800,000 children each year. Over time, federal funding has increased from $96 million when the program began in 1965 to $6.2 billion in 2001.

Head Start is not of the same quality as the model interventions, and the quality varies from center to center. This is partly because Head Start is funded at much lower levels per child than the model programs, and partly because local partners have a lot of say in how individual Head Start centers are run. Head Start costs about 71 percent as much as Perry Preschool, and about 60 percent as much as Carolina Abecedarian. Yet Head Start centers have historically been of higher average quality than other preschool programs available to low-income people. The reason is that, in contrast to the private child-care market, there are few very low-quality Head Start programs.[31]

Some people may be surprised by the claim that Head Start is of relatively high quality. There has been a good deal of publicity about Head Start teachers being grossly underpaid and underqualified, but these claims are unfounded. Discussions of Head Start teacher salaries often ignore the fact that many centers are part-day. Taking into account the number of hours worked shows that on average the hourly wages of Head Start teachers are comparable to those of women with a B.A. degree. Moreover, the vast majority of Head Start teachers have at least an Associates Degree, and in a third of the centers the average teacher has a B.A, and so these teachers are not unqualified.[32]

Head Start is run at the local level according to federal guidelines by grantees that compete for federal funds. Some recent reports about financial irregularities at some Head Start centers are reminiscent of Ronald Reagan's Cadillac-driving welfare "queens." An expose in the *Kansas City Star* reported that one Head Start executive had a $300,000 salary and a leased Mercedes sport-utility vehicle paid for by Head Start funds.[33] In response to these scandals, Congress directed the agency responsible for Head Start to conduct an inquiry into the more than 3,500 local agencies that administer Head Start. This inquiry disclosed only three cases in which Head Start executives were earning more than $230,000 (and 30 percent of that compensation came from sources other than Head Start). The average salary for a Head Start director was only $36,876. Twenty-five agencies spent an average of $356,000 on travel to meetings and conferences, which seems excessive; but most spent only a small fraction of their budgets on travel.[34]

This close examination of Head Start produced very little evidence of financial wrong-doing. Of course, any wrong-doing is disturbing and undermines the program. Head Start grantees should be held accountable for all funds that they receive, and the bad apples should be weeded out of the program. To put things in perspective, we might want to compare the relatively small amount of chicanery in Head Start to the large amount of corruption in areas such as defense procurement. Just this year former Air Force procurement official Darleen Druyun was sentenced to nine months in jail for directing a $23 billion tanker leasing contract to Boeing in return for jobs for herself and other members of her family.[35]

The second common criticism of Head Start is that it doesn't work. Head Start has been attacked as a "scam" because of evidence that initial effects on IQ scores "fade out" over time. The Head Start community has been slow to address this potentially devastating critique. If Head Start is marketed as an "investment" in future child well-being, then it is important to show that it has some lasting effect. The Department of Health and Human Services is currently mounting an experimental evaluation of Head Start, and results from the first year were released in June 2005. In this study, children were randomly assigned either to be in Head Start or not—but many of those who were not in Head Start were in some other preschool. Hence the experiment measures the effect of Head Start relative to the mix of other child-care options available to low-income parents. The early results indicate that Head Start increased the probability that children were in center-based care and improved children's pre-literacy skills and behavior, providing further evidence that Head Start is of high quality relative to the alternatives. Current plans, however, call only for following the children into the early grades, and so the experiment will not address the important issue of whether Head Start has longer-term effects.[36]

The government is also trying to develop a system that would assess the progress of the children in Head Start. In the past, the government has focused exclusively on monitoring the characteristics of Head Start centers. This attempt to come up with "performance measures" for small children has been mired in controversy. One problem is that there is disagreement about exactly what skills should be measured. Should evaluators expect children to master specific academic skills such as saying their ABCs? Or are other skills, such as being able to sit still and listen to a story, more important? A second problem is that it is notoriously difficult to measure accurately the skills of young children. Every parent knows that there is a huge difference between a three-year-old on a good day, and a three-year-old on a bad day. The third, and most intractable, problem is that the Head Start community is deeply suspicious of the current administration's intentions. Many believe that Head Start will be unfairly blamed for deficits in cognitive skills that children brought with them into the program. These people believe that the real aim of the drive for accountability is the destruction of the program.

The lack of information about the outcomes of Head Start children has hampered efforts to assess the program. In a series of studies with Duncan Thomas and other colleagues, I have used national data to try to measure the effect of Head Start. In most of these studies, we compare children who attended Head Start to their own siblings who did not attend. The idea is that siblings share many common background characteristics. By choosing the child's own sibling as a control for the Head Start child, we effectively eliminate the effect of shared family background on child outcomes.

Most previous evaluations of Head Start had focused only on inner-city African American children. While these children are more likely to participate in Head Start than other children, the majority of Head Start children are not black. Because we use national samples, we were able to examine the effects of Head Start among both black and other children. Our first study showed that both black and white Head Start children showed similar gains in vocabulary test scores if we measured them right after the end of Head Start. Among African American children, however, the gains tended to fade out, just as earlier studies of inner-city black children had suggested. In contrast, the white children showed persistent gains in test scores and were less likely to have repeated a grade if they attended Head Start. Subsequent work showed that Hispanic children showed even larger gains from attending Head Start.[37]

Since the initial gains were the same for blacks and whites, this pattern of results suggests first that Head Start does have positive effects for most children. Second, it suggests that Head Start effects do not always "fade out." In fact, our result suggests that "fade out" among black children is likely to be the result of things that happen to these children after they leave Head Start. In subsequent research we showed that black Head Start children went on to attend worse schools than even other black children. So poor schools are an obvious potential explanation for the fade out in Head Start effects. It may be unrealistic to expect a two-year preschool program to serve as an immunization against the future effects of poverty and segregation, especially when those effects include exposure to abysmal inner-city schools.[38]

Only two studies have attempted to follow Head Start children into adulthood. One reports on a group of young adults who participated in Head Start between 1970 and 1971 in Colorado and Florida. These people were compared to a group who had never participated in any form of early childhood education program. To construct the comparison group, the researchers found young adults who had lived on the same streets or neighborhoods as the Head Start children, and who had been enrolled in the same elementary school. In the final sample, however, the Head Start children were still more likely to be from more disadvantaged backgrounds than these neighbors. This finding illustrates one of the critical problems facing any evaluator of Head Start: In any group of poor children, the Head Start program is required to give preference to the children who are neediest. The Colorado/Florida study did not find any statistically significant differences between the two groups of children; but if the Head Start children were worse off to begin with, then even this negative result could be viewed as an accomplishment for the program. We would have expected the Head Start children to do worse than the other children given their backgrounds, but instead they did just as well.[39]

A study that I conducted with Duncan Thomas and Eliana Garces found that Head Start generates long-term improvements in schooling attainment and reductions in crime. The data came from the Panel Study of Income Dynamics (PSID), which began in 1968 with a survey of 4,802 households containing 18,000 individuals. In 1995, adults from the PSID who were age thirty or younger were asked whether they had ever been enrolled in Head Start or any other preschool or day-care program. These adults have been followed since childhood, and they also answered questions about employment, earnings, schooling, and criminal activity. There are roughly 4,000 respondents in the survey who have information both about preschool and about these adult outcomes. Compared to their own siblings, we find that disadvantaged whites who attended Head Start were more likely to graduate from high school and to have attended college. African Americans who attended Head Start were significantly less likely to have been booked or charged with a crime.[40]

In summary, children reap lasting gains from attending Head Start, though the gains are somewhat smaller than those that have been found in "model" programs funded at higher levels. In recent work with Matthew Neidell, I have found that the gains from Head Start increase with per child spending. When we ask which types of spending seem most beneficial, we find that lower pupil-teacher ratios have the greatest impact. This suggests that increasing the per-child funding of the program and reducing pupil-teacher ratios would further improve outcomes. Additional dollars could also be directed toward making the program available to all low-income children. At present, when funds run out, children cannot be served.[41]

A third way to spend Head Start dollars is to extend services to younger children. The Early Head Start (EHS) program was created in 1994 to serve infants and toddlers, and currently about 10 percent of the Head Start budget is spent on these children. Consistent with evaluations of Head Start, those of EHS suggest that it provides child care of generally high quality. Unlike Head Start, EHS has been the subject of a random-assignment evaluation conducted at seventeen sites. As of age three, the treatment children had significantly higher scores on tests of cognitive development, exhibited less aggressive behavior, and showed less negative behavior toward parents during play, and were also better able to devote sustained attention to an object during play than the control children. Given the "fade out" in the effects of Head Start (at least for some children), it will be very important to see how well these gains are maintained over time.[42]

State Preschool Programs

Head Start has served as a model for state preschools targeted to low-income children in places such as California, and also for new (voluntary) universal preschool programs in Georgia, Oklahoma, and New York. Most of these programs have not been properly evaluated, and it is difficult to get information about their quality. Nevertheless, many experts are promoting universal preschool. Even Edward Zigler, the "father" of Head Start, has recently seemed excited by the concept of universal preschool. Whether or not universal pre-K is a good idea depends crucially on whether the programs that are offered are of high quality, and on whether they serve the disadvantaged children who have most to gain from these programs.

If the programs are run by failing urban school districts, then it is hard to imagine that they will be of higher quality than the elementary schools run by these same districts. One recent analysis of kindergarten children found that those who had been enrolled in state-sponsored preschools did significantly better than those who had been in Head Start, who in turn did better than those who had not attended any preschool. But the children in the state-sponsored preschools also had the highest average family incomes, which suggests that these state programs were not successfully targeting the neediest children.[43]

Even if universal programs do enroll all of the neediest children, it will still be the case that many more affluent parents receive large child-care subsidies through these programs. There is nothing wrong with subsidizing higher-income parents (as we already do through the Dependent Care Tax Credit, or the mortgage interest deduction), though it is legitimate to question whether this is the best use of scarce tax dollars. Nevertheless we should recognize that many if not most affluent children will attend preschool in any case, and that there is little hard evidence that affluent children benefit from attending preschool to the same extent as low-income children.

Of course, given the low average quality of the care available today in most centers, it is possible that a high-quality universal pre-K program would improve the quality of care available to even high-income children, and this might have some social benefit. This does not seem to have happened in the Canadian province of Quebec, where a universal, five-dollars-per-day preschool system was introduced in 1993. Instead of creating a network of high-quality centers, the government had to scramble to offer enough subsidized places to meet the demand and ended up using many loosely regulated providers. Michael Baker, Jonathan Gruber, and Kevin Milligan find that the expanded network of centers made children worse off in several health and behavior-related dimensions.[44]

A second argument that is sometimes made in support of a universal program is that it is necessary to propose a universal program in order to create the political support necessary to provide child care for low-income children. The argument then is that affluent parents will not support child-care programs that are aimed primarily at benefitting low-income children. The existence of Head Start provides a counterargument, though perhaps the program's current political problems underline how difficult it is to get wealthy people to subsidize the poor over the longer term.

New Jersey has taken an innovative approach to the issue of providing high-quality care for low-income children as a result of a long-running law suit, *Abbott vs. Burke*. In 1998, the state Supreme Court ordered the state to establish preschool programs in thirty needy, mostly urban, school districts. In 2000, the state Department of Education mandated that the districts provide full-day preschool. The "Abbott program" now enrolls 43,000 students in high-quality child-care centers. In fact, the court took the unprecedented step of defining quality by mandating pupil-teacher ratios, staff qualifications, and access to special services, if needed. In terms of these measurable aspects of quality, the Abbott program centers now look better than many Head Start centers in New Jersey. Yet this judicial solution has not been without controversy— several school districts are currently pursuing a lawsuit against the state because the state has not fully financed the cost of running these centers.[45] Still, the Abbott program represents a promising direction for state initiatives, because it targets scarce child-care dollars to the children who need it most, and provides high-quality programming.

In California, Proposition 10 specifies that money from a tax on tobacco be used to expand preschool availability, with the eventual stated aim of implementing a universal preschool program. Implementation of the program varies from county to county. In Los Angeles, programs that have applied for funding are being rated by trained observers—only programs that score at least three stars on a five-star scale will receive funding. At least some funding will be used to provide space to low-income children who might not otherwise be able to attend. As in New Jersey, this program is focused both on improving the quality of preschool and on making sure that low-income children have a chance to enroll. It will be important to assess the extent to which it is able to meet these two important goals.[46]

Out-of-School Care for Older Children

Older children also need out-of-school care. Between 1997 and 2002, the U.S. Department of Education increased funding for 21st Century Community Learning Centers, which are school-based after-school programs, from $40 million to $1 billion. In 2001, 1.2 million elementary and middle school students participated in this program in 3,600 schools. State governments have also increased their spending. In California, Proposition 49 potentially increased state funding for before- and after-school programs up to $455 million dollars, beginning in 2004, although this mandate will not take effect until the state has climbed out of its current budget hole. Proponents of the measure argued that up to a million California children under the age of fifteen were left unsupervised after school, and that after-school programs could reduce crime rates by 40 percent or more.[47]

Despite these problems, a national survey of after-school programs showed that existing program were underutilized—enrollments were at an average of only 59 percent of the capacity of licensed programs, and only one-third of programs were operating at 75 percent or more of capacity. The widespread perception that after-school programs are unavailable seems to be incorrect, though it is of course possible that existing programs are undersubscribed because they are too expensive, or because they are not meeting the needs of children and parents. In the 2000 competition for the 21st Century Community Learning Centers, 2,252 communities applied for funds that were sufficient to fund only 310 grantees.[48]

This national survey also reported that 90 percent of the before-school enrollments, and 83 percent of the after-school enrollments are of children in pre-kindergarten through grade three, so that the programs are not used very much for the older children who are most at risk of being left on their own. Fewer than half of all programs offer creative writing, sports, field trips, or science activities at least once a week. Quality is very uneven, with some programs employing high school dropouts, and maintaining ratios of twenty-five children to one teacher.

Most evaluations of after-school programs focus on model programs that offer tutoring. For example, the Howard Street Tutoring Program randomly assigned second and third grade students with poor reading scores to a treatment group that received tutoring, or to a control group. The treatment group showed improvements in basal word recognition and spelling.

The L.A.'s Best program has also received a great deal of attention. This program offers comprehensive after-school tutoring, cultural enrichment, recreation, computer, and nutrition services to kindergarten and elementary school children in nineteen of Los Angeles's poorest schools. Three studies have compared the L.A.'s Best children to control children drawn from the same schools. There is some evidence that the L.A.'s Best children did better in certain respects than the controls—but many of the analyses are flawed. For instance, Denise Huang and her colleagues report increases in the Stanford 9 test scores of L.A.'s Best children, but does not compare them to Stanford 9 test scores of other children. This is a potentially important omission, as test scores in the Los Angeles Unified School District have shown overall increases in recent years—between 1998–99 and 2000–2001 the mean percentile on the Stanford 9 reading increased from 27 to 38 for second-grade students.[49]

There have been few evaluations of programs aimed at keeping older children in school and out of trouble. The Quantum Opportunities program randomly assigned ninth grade students who were on public assistance either to a control group, or to a treatment group that engaged in after-school educational activities and community service activities each year for four years. Treatment students received monetary rewards for completing each portion of the program. Participants in this program were more likely to graduate from high school or to obtain a GED than controls, and they were more likely to go on to post-secondary education. They also had significantly fewer children and reported being more hopeful about the future than other teens. But there was no significant difference in the probability that participants had been "in trouble with police" in the past year.

Big Brothers/Big Sisters has been shown to be effective in improving a range of outcomes. For example, it reduces the probability that a little brother or sister hits someone or starts taking drugs, and improves schooling attendance. The "I Have a Dream" program, which pays college tuition if children graduate from high school, has had large impacts on high school graduation.[50]

These model programs show that it is possible to make a difference in the lives of school-aged children. Yet these intensive, expensive, privately funded programs bear little resemblance to the after-school programs available to most children, and cannot even be regarded primarily as child-care programs. At this point, it is a leap of faith to argue that the average after-school program has any effect on child outcomes, or that it reduces crime.[51]

A recent evaluation of the 21st Century Learning Program reinforces this conclusion. This evaluation included a large number of both elementary and middle school children. Twenty-six programs serving elementary students were assessed using random assignment. A national sample of programs for middle school children was assessed by creating a matched sample of control children to compare to the program children. One of the more startling conclusions of the evaluation is that the program had no impact on the number of latch-key children or on children's academic achievement. The elementary school children did report feeling safer, though the middle-school children did not. Most of these programs offered homework assistance and enriching activities, and so given the rhetoric surrounding the importance of after-school programs, it is surprising that they did not have more impact. One possible explanation is that on average, most students attended only two days a week. Another possibility is that some types of programs were more effective than others, and that these programs have not yet been identified. The most reasonable conclusion, however, is that the quality of typical after-school programs will have to be upgraded significantly before they can be expected to have impacts similar to those of model programs.[52]

Summary

Good-quality child care is a vital aspect of the safety net for poor children. Nobel laureate James Heckman argues that quality child-care programs are in fact one of *the* most effective ways to help these children because "skill begets skill." He also argues that, unfortunately, America underinvests in the education and care of young children relative to what it spends on training adults.[53] The most serious problem with many public efforts to supply child care—for example, through voucher programs—is that the importance of quality has been ignored.

The most notable exception to this generalization is Head Start, which has maintained generally high-quality programs for poor children for almost forty years. One reason that Head Start is of higher quality than many state efforts is that Head Start has always had the goal of helping children, rather than supporting work. While supporting work is a worthy goal, it should be obvious that given a fixed budget, one can either provide many places of low quality (and allow many women to work), or provide fewer child-care places that are of higher quality. Hence there is a tension between state efforts to support work and efforts to improve child-care quality. Generally, the goal of supporting work by creating many child care places has won out. Programs that focus on supporting work by subsidizing child care of low quality may be harming children in the long run, and certainly represent a missed opportunity to help all children reach their potential.

In chapter 4, I argued that the government should stop providing actual housing units and switch to a voucher program. In this chapter, I am arguing that public provision of child care through Head Start has historically worked better than vouchers (which is what child-care subsidies are). While these positions may seem contradictory, a key difference between the housing market and the child-care market is in the relative effectiveness of regulation. The federal government is not in a position to regulate child care, and many states have chosen to set quality floors at a very low level. States may never have the resources or the will effectively to police child-care quality in family homes or other informal child-care settings.

In contrast, Section 8 vouchers provide an incentive for landlords to upgrade their housing. The federal government also gives money to local housing authorities that is used to pay for the inspections necessary to insure that subsidized housing meets Section 8 standards. If the federal government adopted similar policies with respect to child care, it would make state block grants for child care contingent on the quality of care provided, and impose much higher standards than many states have adopted. Failing this, the best way for the federal government to intervene in the child-care market is through the expansion of Head Start, where it does have some control of the quality of care provided by its grantees.

Chapter 6

Defending and Mending the Safety Net

Government's view of the economy could be summed up in
a few short phrases: If it moves, tax it. If it keeps moving,
regulate it. And if it stops moving, subsidize it.
—Ronald Reagan in "Remarks to the White House
Conference on Small Business", August 15, 1986.

There are good and concrete theoretical reasons to argue for the
role of government in alleviating poverty. One of the most important arguments in favor of government involvement is the existence
of "market failures"—something that prevents free markets from
providing the efficient allocation of resources. Take Nobel Laureate
Milton Friedman's explanation of why private charity may never be
sufficient to deal with the problem of poverty alleviation. In "Capitalism and Freedom," Friedman argues that all individuals benefit
from all charity—their own as well as their neighbors'. As he put it,
"It can be argued that private charity is insufficient because the
benefits from it accrue to people other than those who make the
gifts. . . . I am distressed by the sight of poverty; I am benefitted by
its alleviation; but I am benefitted equally whether I or someone else
pays for its alleviation."[1] Ultimately, it doesn't matter *who* takes care
of the poor as long as *someone* does, which tends to lead people to
"free-ride" on the efforts of others, resulting in too little private

charity. How many times have you heard about a program doing wonderful work, felt briefly inspired to offer your support, and then neglected to mail that check? Well, you're no outlier.

The same dynamic is at work in the provision of aid to poor families and children. Most acknowledge that the poor need some sort of help, but without government intervention it's unlikely that private citizens will ever meet all of the need.

There's another argument for government intervention. Even well-meaning parents do not always make the optimal investments in their children. Some parents can't afford to. They are subject to "liquidity constraints" that prevent parents from being able to borrow money to pay for investments (such as checkups, good nutrition, and fine schools) that would have a payoff for their children down the road. Other parents may not value the benefits that would accrue to society as a whole when children achieve their full potential. In this case, parents have not fully internalized the "externality" involved when children do something of benefit (or that imposes a cost) to those outside the family. Finally, parents may not always know the best thing to do. In the preceding chapters we have seen examples of imperfect information problems in, for example, the market for child care. This isn't to say that government can make optimal choices, but it can offer to support some minimal requirements.

It is one thing to make a theoretical case for government intervention, and something entirely different to argue that government programs are in fact effective. Thus, the most straightforward line of attack against safety net programs has been to argue that they are simply ineffective—that they must be ineffective. As a graduate student at Princeton, I was struck by a professor's comment that we should think of government as an entity that takes tax dollars and dumps them in the ocean. The view that government (or at least the federal government) is incapable of solving problems is strongly held in America.

The resurgence in this view puts the federal safety net at a crossroads. There are three options for the reform of the safety net, which we considered in the introduction. The first is to dismantle it and give the money to the states. The evidence in this book shows that this would not make the average poor person better off. The programs that would be destroyed are generally doing what they were intended to do, though there is certainly much room for improvement. At the same time, some programs that have been established at the state or local level (e.g., SCHIP, child-care subsidies, housing construction programs) have run into problems with funding, low quality of services, and/or a failure to target the truly needy, suggesting that devolution is not a panacea for the problems of the poor, as appealing as it may be to some political constituencies.

A second option is to reform the existing individual programs. This would certainly be more desirable than dismantling the safety net, especially because we now know a great deal about how the programs could be improved, as the preceding chapters have discussed. As effective as these reforms could be, however, piecemeal reform would not address systemic problems, such as the lack of co-ordination among programs and the fact that many eligibles find it too costly to take up their benefits.

Reform of the existing programs may be the most that can be achieved in the current political environment—but the preferred option would involve a more radical reform that would provide universal, coordinated benefits to low-income children. While such a vision may seem utopian in the United States today, it is the norm in many European countries. Even if, like Moses, advocates of systemic reform find themselves wandering in a (political) wilderness for many years, it is still helpful to have a vision of how the promised land might look.

Attacks on the Safety Net

The argument that safety net programs don't work is not new. The late President Ronald Reagan often made this argument humorously, as in the opening quotation. Reagan's jokes, however, were accompanied by action. Many of the programs described in this book suffered dramatic cuts under the Reagan administration and some have never recovered to pre-Reagan levels of real funding. For example, as discussed in chapter 4, funding for housing programs fell from $75 billion in 1978 to $16 billion by 1983.

In 1981, the Reagan administration increased the "benefit reduction ratio" for the AFDC program. Instead of losing $0.67 in benefits for each dollar of earnings, women on AFDC now lost $1.00 of benefits for each dollar of earnings. The practical effect was that women became ineligible for assistance from AFDC at much lower levels of earnings. Robert Moffitt calculated that before this change, women with incomes of up to $612 per month (in 1982 dollars) were eligible for some assistance from AFDC. After the change, this "breakeven" level of earnings fell to $394 per month. Not surprisingly, participation in the program fell from 53 percent of all single mothers to 44 percent within one year.[2]

It was also in 1981 that Reagan's budget director, David Stockman, infamously proposed counting ketchup as a vegetable in the school lunch program to make it cheaper for school districts to satisfy the program's nutritional requirements. This proposal was widely decried as mean-spirited and fortunately was not passed into law. Nonetheless, legislation that reduced reimbursements for the school breakfast program and tightened income eligibility guidelines for school lunches was passed. Enrollments in the school lunch program fell by 2.9 million children between 1981 and 1982 while enrollments in school breakfast fell by half a million children. Enrollments did not begin to recover until some of these changes were rescinded in 1986.[3]

These cuts in the federal safety net occurred as America entered the deepest recession since World War II. Unemployment rates hovered above 9.5 percent during 1982 and 1983. Ironically, the bad economic situation masked some of the cuts in the generosity of safety net programs—while the programs became less generous, more people became poor enough meet the stricter eligibility requirements. We have seen a similar phenomenon in the most recent recession. For example, Medicaid and SCHIP provided health insurance for about four million people who would otherwise have become uninsured during the economic downturn of 2001 and 2002.[4]

The Reagan administration was able to make these cuts because many people believed that the programs had failed. The programs were sold to the public as part of a "War on Poverty" that began in the 1960s. But while anti-poverty programs for the elderly (such as Social Security and Medicare) had dramatic measurable effects on poverty among the elderly, programs for children and families did not seem to be having any impact. Children remain the poorest demographic group in America, and the fraction of children who are poor has changed little over the past thirty years: In 2001, 15.8 percent of children were poor compared to 15.1 percent in 1971.[5]

Many years later, the same impulse, fueled by public dissatisfaction with welfare programs for poor women and children, led the Clinton administration to "end welfare as we know it." Today, the perception that the programs don't work continues to undermine public support for the safety net.

This book shows that on the contrary, safety net programs not only work but have significant effects on the well-being of children. Why then, has there been so little movement in official poverty statistics? The official poverty rate counts only cash income and excludes programs that provide benefits like health care, food stamps, and EITC benefits. By definition then, even the most generous non-cash programs have little impact on official poverty rates simply because they're not included in the official statistics. Since aid to families with children has been increasingly offered in the form of these non-cash benefits, the benefits to children are not measured by official statistics.

This problem has long been recognized in both academic and policy circles. In 1998, the Center for Budget and Policy Priorities estimated that cash transfers to families with children lifted 2.2 million children out of poverty. Safety net programs would have lifted about 5.3 million children out of poverty had they been counted.[6] The National Research Council of the National Academy of Sciences published a report on the measurement of poverty in 1995, which recommended that the definition of poverty be changed to reflect all of the resources available to the household, rather than focusing exclusively on cash income. The Census bureau concluded that implementing the proposed measure would reduce the gap in poverty rates between children and adults, because in-kind programs and the EITC have a greater impact on children than on others.[7]

I do not mean to imply that the problem of continuing child poverty is simply one of mismeasurement. The Census bureau concluded that even using the proposed new measure of poverty, a quarter of U.S. children were poor. My point is that because of the safety net, even the poor are less wretched than they would be otherwise. Poor people with access to food, housing, and medicine provided by government programs are better off than similarly poor people without those benefits. There is nothing shocking in this assertion, but it's a point that's often ignored.

I also recognize that the existing programs are imperfect. The preceding chapters are filled with specific criticisms and suggestions for reform; but a realistic assessment of the strengths and weaknesses of current safety net programs shows that by and large they are doing the job they were created to do. Addressing their documented shortcomings would be more constructive, if less glamorous, than scrapping them and starting over with a new set of untested programs. I suspect that new programs would be rolled out with great fanfare but would promptly begin to experience many of the same problems that plague current programs. If, that is, the new programs ever made it past discussion in various Congressional committees or state legislatures.

This brings me to a second line of attack against the safety net, which is the argument that anti-poverty programs should be administered at the state rather than at the federal level. This argument underlies recent attempts to "block-grant" many safety net programs. Under a block grant, the money that is spent on federal programs would be given to the states, with few strings attached.

This idea also has a long history. In 1981, the Reagan administration proposed converting the Medicaid program into a system of block grants. In 1995, a similar Medicaid proposal passed both the

House of Representatives and the Senate but was vetoed by President Clinton. A proposal by the same Congress to block-grant all federal food and nutrition programs also failed. In 2003 the Bush administration proposed a similar plan that would combine federal payments to states for hospitals, Medicaid, and the State Children's Health Insurance Program into a single fixed annual block payment to states that would be capped. State changes to the programs (such as restrictions on benefits or charges for services) would no longer require federal permission, and states would not be required to "match" federal dollars.[8] This particular proposal has not gone anywhere because states understand that it would mean less and less federal help with the rising cost of providing medical care to the poor over time.

Bush administration proposals to block-grant public housing programs have also been beaten back. After being defeated in Congress, however, the Bush administration has gone through administrative channels to cut housing voucher programs. It has issued new administrative guidelines saying that it will cap the federal contribution to vouchers at the level of August 2003 (adjusted for inflation) regardless of the actual level of rents. This will force local housing authorities either to serve fewer families or to offer them smaller vouchers.[9] The *New York Times* concluded, "Having paid lip service to the goal of ending chronic homelessness, the Bush administration is now threatening to kill off the only program [Section 8] that could possibly achieve it."[10]

The debate over Head Start reauthorization illustrates starkly different positions with regard to the potential role of the federal government in ameliorating poverty.[11] As of 2005, a proposal to completely eliminate Head Start and give the money to states in the form of block grants had been defeated, but Head Start was still up for reauthorization. On July 25, 2003, the House of Representatives passed, by a single vote, a bill that could lead to the gradual elimination of the program. The bill "block-grants" Head Start in eight states. In these states, the bill envisages that money that would have gone to Head Start will be given to state governors. The state governors will not be required to fund child care that adheres to any performance standards and will be allowed to use block grant funds rather than welfare TANF funds to pay for child care. In other words, the bill would give more money to states without actually requiring them to spend more on quality child care rather than, for example, subsidies to unregulated care.

The full Senate has not voted on Head Start reauthorization, but the bill that has come out of the relevant subcommittee does not include block grants, and does increase funding for Head Start by $400 million per year. The bill increases eligibility for Head Start to 130 percent of the poverty line and requires the Health and Human Services Secretary to develop standards for evaluating the progress of Head Start students that are in accordance with recommendations made by an expert panel of the National Research Council. This bill would, however, require programs to "recompete" for funds every five years.

Little economic rationale has been offered for moving antipoverty programs from the federal to the state level. In contrast, there are compelling arguments against these proposals. First, as we have seen, many federal safety net programs like Head Start and public housing are actually already administered locally but subject to federal standards. Moving control of the programs to state governments would involve more, rather than less, bureaucracy, and in many cases, would involve the elimination of federal standards in favor of much weaker state standards.

As Carlos Jackson, the executive director of the Los Angeles County Community Development Commission, argued in federal testimony against the housing block grant proposal,

> [T]he block grant proposal would add an additional layer of bureaucracy by transferring the Section 8 program to states. There has been no evidence presented to suggest that state administration would lead to a more efficient and effective program. In fact, it is interesting to note that 40 percent of state administered housing authorities are rated as "troubled" by HUD's own scoring system (SEMAP). Conversely only eight percent of locally administered Section 8 programs are

similarly rated. . . . This just doesn't make sense. Our question continues to go unanswered by HUD: Why punish the well performing [local] agencies?

Mr. Jackson finished by saying, "[O]ne can only conclude that the intent of HANF is to either strategically gut the program or to relieve the federal government of its role in providing affordable housing."[12]

A key difference between the federal government and most state governments is that the federal government can run a deficit. Traditionally, the national government increases spending in bad times to provide a boost to the economy—this has been a prominent rationale for the Bush administration tax cuts. Safety-net programs act as automatic stabilizers to the economy. Spending on these programs goes up as bad times make more families eligible. When good times return, spending falls. In contrast, states bound by balanced-budget statutes must cut spending when revenue falls. This means that state-funded safety net programs are apt to fail precisely when they are most needed.

Recent cuts to state Medicaid and SCHIP programs are a prime example of this process. In recent years, virtually every state legislature in the country was considering cuts to the Medicaid and SCHIP programs to balance the budget. In 2003, rule changes pushed more than 49,000 low-income children off the SCHIP rolls in Texas alone. Florida stopped enrolling new applicants in its SCHIP program and has built up a waiting list of 100,000 children. California has also proposed freezing enrollment in SCHIP, which would affect approximately 114,000 children. The Center on Budget and Policy Priorities estimates that between 1.2 and 1.6 million people, half of them children, may lose eligibility for public health insurance due to budget cuts. Those who remain eligible for public health insurance face reductions in benefits, increased cost sharing, waiting periods (e.g., children in Texas must wait three months after enrollment before receiving services) and doctors who are refusing to serve them because of low reimbursements.[13] At a time when the number of uninsured is rapidly rising, the state programs meant to serve them are shrinking, and some states, such as Missouri, may choose to opt out of these programs altogether. This makes devolution through block granting supremely unappealing—unless, that is, one's goal is to dismantle the social safety net altogether.

It is true that states have not yet been compelled to cut back on their TANF spending, and that TANF is the most prominent example of devolution to date. This is largely because states were able to divert much of the TANF block grant to child-care spending before the downturn. Then, when the inevitable downturn arrived, states cut back on child-care spending, as we saw in chapter 5.

The third and most compelling argument against block grants is the idea that there should be a uniform, minimum standard of living for children, regardless of what part of the country they live in. Why should a child born in Mississippi have fewer rights (as measured in federal spending) than one born in New York? While there are differences in the cost of living across regions, these differences are much smaller than the differences in state funding for anti-poverty programs. Federal safety net programs help raise living standards in the poorest states. At issue is whether "states' rights" are more important than children's rights to adequate food, shelter, and medical care. If we truly believe that every American child should have access to basic necessities, then it makes sense for the federal government to specify minimum standards—and the federal government must also make sure that even the poorest states have the resources to provide this safety net.

Considerable evidence also suggests that spending levels in one state influence spending in neighboring states. Having one state slash benefits can set off a regional "race to the bottom" since no state wants to attract poor households from out of state by having higher benefit levels than its neighbors.[14]

That the federal government can run deficits is an argument in favor of retaining control of anti-poverty programs at the federal level. But the ballooning federal deficit is itself one of the greatest immediate threats to the safety net. Baldly stated, if the deficit continues to grow, there will be no money left for anti-poverty pro-grams for children. William Gale and Laurence Kotlikoff point out that recent tax cuts (e.g., the tax cut of 2001 is estimated to cost $187 billion in 2010), proposals to make the tax cuts permanent, and the new Medicare prescription drug benefit (estimated to cost $40 billion per year) will have to be paid for somehow. They esti-mate that these increases in spending (decreases in revenue) are so large that to offset them would require the following: a 53 percent cut in Social Security benefits; a 63 percent cut in Medicare bene-fits; the complete elimination of federal spending on Medicaid; a 38 percent increase in payroll taxes (e.g., income taxes); or a 58 per-cent cut in all spending other than interest on the national debt, de-fense, and homeland security.[15]

In this new fiscal regime there will be enormous pressure to cut virtually all federal government programs. Safety net programs for children are particularly vulnerable because they are discretionary programs that need to be periodically reauthorized. That is, the programs are authorized for a specific period, and then require a new act of Congress to keep them going. While it is still unclear which programs will be cut, and how much, the debate is already well underway. In March 2004, the Senate approved a budget reso-lution calling for reductions of $117 billion over five years in virtu-ally all discretionary domestic federal programs. Under this resolu-tion, spending on these programs would fall from 3.3 percent of GDP today, to 2.7 percent of GDP by 2009. Moreover, the Senate budget plan left out any spending on the war in Iraq after 2005, suggesting that the actual budget cuts required to pay for the war, tax cuts, and the Medicare prescription drug benefit will have to be even greater.[16]

Given these fiscal realities, Congress was not even able to agree on a budget in 2004. Perhaps proven programs for children can be saved by taking a hard look at unproven programs such as Missile Defense ($10.2 billion for 2005), farm subsidies averaging $1,000,000 per full-time farm ($19 billion per year), or tax subsidies to home owners ($100.4 billion per year).[17] Congress, however, appears to be moving in the other direction. In October 2004, Congress approved $136 billion in tax cuts for businesses, including special cuts for operators of NASCAR race tracks, makers of bows and arrows, and importers of ceiling fans, among other special interests. All told, the bill included 276 provisions for specific groups.[18]

Americans must make hard choices, something they're not terribly good at. In a critique of federal nutrition programs, conservative commentator Douglas Besharov wrote that "liberal advocacy groups . . . seem to believe that admitting any weaknesses in federal feeding programs would make those programs vulnerable to budget cuts."[19] Under the circumstances, such beliefs may be well founded. It would not be unreasonable to conclude that proposals to scale back or block-grant safety net programs actually reflect a desire to eliminate the safety net altogether, as Senator Moynihan feared.

One popular and compelling argument for the abolition of these programs is that parents know what is best for their children. It follows then that putting more money into the hands of parents is the best way to help children. This argument ignores the minority of parents who do not do right by their children—parents who are drug addicted, violent, ill-informed about their children's needs, or otherwise unable to be good parents—and we must not forget these children. Even well-meaning parents who care about their children will not spend every penny of a cash transfer on their children. Consider that the recent $600 tax cut led to a spike in sales of consumer durables such as refrigerators and washing machines, as well as cars.

Even if parents had only their child's best interests at heart and spent every penny of any additional income that they received on their child, the evidence in this book suggests that the money saved by eliminating safety net programs would have little effect on child outcomes. If current programs were eliminated and the money was transferred to all parents with children, then parents could expect to receive payments of $1,488 per child, per year. This is not sufficient to allow poor families to purchase medical insurance, adequate housing, nutritious food, and quality child care.[20] For example, Head Start alone spends about $4,500 per child per year on the children enrolled in its programs. Alternatively, if the programs were eliminated and the tax savings were distributed over all tax pay-ers (rather than only to families with children), then poor families could expect to receive very little. In contrast, the programs that these tax dollars support have made a significant difference in the lives of many poor children.

A Proposal for Systemic Reform

Viewed as a system, the safety net programs highlighted in this book do a remarkable job of helping children. Yet the system—insofar as it *is* a system—has patchwork coverage, obvious inequities, and ad-ministrative complexity. Perhaps a clear recognition of what our welfare system has become will provide the impetus for reform. Jonathon Swift savaged the colonial administration of Ireland with his tongue-in-cheek recommendation that the Irish be encouraged to eat their children. In America we are faced with a complex wel-fare system that often helps but sometimes does devour needy chil-dren. To reform the system, we need to keep three principles in mind.

First, the welfare system should target necessary services to the needy. Some aspects of public assistance have an "all or nothing" quality. Either you win the lottery and receive a high level of services or you lose and receive nothing at all. For example, housing pro-grams serve only a fraction of eligible families, and cuts to Medic-aid/SCHIP are being enacted by dropping children from the rolls. We need to ensure that every child receives at least a minimum level of necessary goods and services. Aid must not be all-or-nothing, but should be graduated to offer a minimum standard for all children.

Second, we must coordinate and simplify eligibility requirements across programs. Complex eligibility requirements discourage participation by the neediest families, are costly to administer, and make it harder to detect fraud. If it is almost impossible for an outside observer to decipher the program rules, how can an administrator be expected to determine accurately whether or not someone is breaking them?

Third, the welfare system should encourage rather than discourage work and self-sufficiency. The long-term viability of any welfare system requires public acceptance, and the American public will not accept a system that encourages dependence on public programs and does not require any effort from its participants.

A system that would meet these objectives could be constructed along the following lines:

1. Make every child eligible for a core set of benefits, including child care and housing vouchers, specified medical services, and food and nutrition programs.
2. Charge for these benefits using a sliding fee scale where the poorest pay nothing, people with more money pay a modest fee, and those above a cutoff pay market value.
3. Collect the fees through the income tax system.
4. Allow families to opt out of using and paying for the publicly provided services.

I envisage each family receiving an electronic card that they could use to access a range of services. Families that wished to opt out of the program altogether would just cut up their card. If, by the end of the year, they had never activated it, then they would not be charged any fees. Families who wished to access some programs and not others could do so—providers would enter a unique code for each type of program activated in a central database. At the end of the year, taxpayers would receive a form like a W2 showing which programs, if any, they had accessed. The final fees assessed would depend on their taxable income.

In many ways, this proposal codifies existing practice. The government already specifies a minimum bundle of services that poor children are eligible to receive. The problem is that for some programs, such as public housing and Head Start, there are not enough places for all those eligible. In the case of public housing, I argued in chapter 4, this problem could be solved by "voucherizing" the program. In the case of Head Start, the problem might be solved either by increasing funding for the existing program or by providing vouchers enabling children to attend other high-quality preschools.

Programs such as food stamps have pioneered electronic cards and have shown that they can be a practical way to administer benefits. A similar proposal has been made in connection with Social Security reform—that employers make enrollment in 401(k) plans automatic unless workers choose to opt out.[21]

The second proposal, to charge sliding fees, is bound to be more controversial. The government has already adopted this principal with respect to the expansion of children's health insurance under the SCHIP program. In most states, families eligible for Medicaid are not required to pay a fee, while those with slightly higher incomes are eligible for SCHIP and pay a modest premium. The principal of "free and reduced price" meals has also been part of the school lunch and breakfast programs, and clients of public housing programs pay fees based on their ability to pay. Hence, there is nothing radical about extending the concept of sliding fees to the full range of safety net programs.

The introduction of sliding fees for all safety net programs would help to reduce the work disincentives inherent in the welfare system by eliminating steep "cliffs." By a cliff, I mean a point where earning an additional dollar of income causes benefits to fall to zero. Under the current system, a family that earns a dollar more than the Medicaid income threshold, for example, loses eligibility for the program. So earning a dollar more can cost a family hundreds of dollars in benefits. With sliding fees, the value of benefits would decline more gradually with income. Sliding fees do not entirely eliminate work disincentives, since those who work more still receive fewer benefits. With sliding fees, however, families would no longer face huge decreases in their income with small increases in work effort. By adjusting the fees, the government could also make eligibility more uniform across programs, rather than having different cutoffs for every program.

The third proposal, to charge fees through the tax system, is also likely to be unpopular, not least with the Internal Revenue Service. Here again, however, the government has already made the IRS an integral part of the welfare system by making it the administrator of the EITC, one of the government's largest anti-poverty programs.

Hence, to charge the IRS with collecting fees for other welfare programs would expand the IRS role, rather than change it in any fundamental way. The EITC makes a program of this type possible by giving poor as well as non-poor people a reason to file tax returns. In the past, a person with very low earnings had little reason to file a tax return at all. Now, most families eligible for the EITC file a return, which makes it possible to administer other safety net programs through the tax system.

Countries with a universal child allowance system (such as Canada and Great Britain) recoup some of the money spent on well-off children through the tax system. That is, if the allowance is viewed as taxable income, then people in a 50 percent tax bracket will end up paying half of the credit back to the government. The sliding fees proposal goes further since it would be possible to charge fees to high-income parents that covered the cost of the services provided to their children, and/or subsidized services for low-income children.

The most controversial aspect of the proposal is likely to be the idea of making every child eligible, but this is the key to improving services for poor children. Under the current system, the parents of poor children must repeatedly prove their eligibility. Under the proposed system, poor children would get benefits automatically and parents of non-poor children would have to take action to decline benefits that they did not want.

The problem with the current system is that poor parents are often the least able to negotiate complex administrative requirements. Moreover, extending eligibility to all children would significantly reduce administrative complexity. While having to take action to decline public benefits might aggravate some well-off parents, the cost to them would be very small, while the benefits to the poor would be large. Automatic eligibility would remove a key barrier to the use of safety net programs and bring us closer to the goal of serving every child.

While it has become an article of faith that "big government" is the cause of many of our ills, this book shows that most safety net programs for poor children do a remarkable job. Dismantling the safety net would cause severe hardship and undermine the progress that has been made in bringing the poorest children up to a minimum level of access to important services. In the short term, safety net programs should be defended and reformed, using existing and continuing research as a guide. In the long term, safety net programs need to be more effectively integrated and targeted at the most vulnerable children in our society.

This chapter offers one proposal for systemic reform. Such reform would take the patchwork pieces of our current safety net and turn them into a quilt that would enfold our children from birth to adulthood. It is perhaps politically naïve to raise the profile of the invisible safety net and to discuss the integration of its programs at a time when it is under increasing attack. Many parts of the safety net have survived and grown by relying on support from other constituencies such as the farm lobby, teachers, or those in favor of urban renewal, rather than by making a direct appeal to legislators for the welfare of our children. We regularly hear that "our children are our future." If we truly believe this, then we must serve them better than we have.

I am sometimes asked why (non-poor) people should care about poor children. This book lays out the argument that ignoring the problems of the poor is "penny-wise but pound-foolish." I show that there are cost-effective ways to intervene in the lives of poor children, and argue that these interventions will benefit all of society in the long run.

A more fundamental argument is not one of cost-effectiveness, however, but of morals. President George Bush stated the issue eloquently in his 2001 inaugural address:

> America, at its best, is compassionate. In the quiet of the American conscience, we know that deep, persistent poverty is unworthy of our nation's promise. . . . Where there is suffering, there is duty. Americans in need are not strangers, they are citizens, not problems, but priorities. And all of us are diminished when

any are hopeless. . . . And I can pledge our nation to a goal: When we see that wounded traveler on the road to Jericho, we will not pass to the other side.

As a nation we must stop passing by on the other side. We must act to fulfill the pledge to make poor children a national priority by reforming and expanding the invisible safety net that supports them.

TABLE 1

Expenditures and Caseloads for Safety Net Programs, 2002

	Expenditures (billions)	Caseload (millions)
Cash		
TANF payments	**13**	5.1
Other TANF services	**8.5**	NA
Earned Income Tax Credit	**27.8**	19.8
Total Supplemental Security Income (SSI)	38.5	6.8
SSI (children)	**5.2**	0.9
Health Care		
Total Medicaid	258.2	42.8
Medicaid (children and non-disabled adults)	**44.6**	28.5
SCHIP	5.4	5.7
Nutrition		
Total Food Stamps	24.1	19.1
Food Stamps (families with children)	**13**	10.3
School Lunch	**6.1**	16
WIC	**4.4**	7.5
School Breakfast	**1.5**	6.7
Housing		
Low-Rent Public Housing	8.9	1.3
Section 8 and other assisted rental housing	25.2	3.7*
Tenant-based vouchers (2001)	[16.7]	[1.8]
Low-Income Housing Tax Credit	[5.1]	[1.1]
Homeless programs	1.4	NA

TABLE 1 (*continued*)

	Expenditures (billions)	Caseload (millions)
Housing Block Grants	1.5	NA
USDA Rural programs	9.3	NA
Approx. total for families with children	**23.8**	NA
Child Care		
Child Care and Development Block Grant	**8.6**	1.8
Head Start	**8.2**	0.9
Total Expenditures for Children:	**170.1**	
Cash Welfare Payments as %Total:	**8%**	

Notes: Expenditures include federal, state, and local spending except for housing programs where many tax subsidies are excluded. Sum is of bolded expenditures. The main source is U.S. House of Representatives, Committee on Ways and Means, *2004 Green Book*, doc. no. 13-35-13-41 (Washington, D.C.: U.S. Government Printing Office, 2004): See tables 3-14, 7-6, 9-16, 13-14, 15-2, 15-8, 15-12, 15-21, 15-25, 15-26, 15-27, 15-28, Chart 15-3, and pages K10–K12. See also Millennial Housing Commission, "Meeting Our Nation's Housing Challenges: Report of the Bipartisan Millennial Housing Commission Appointed by the Congress of the United States," Washington, D.C., 2002: appendix 3; appendix 1, table 6; and http://www.huduser.org/datasets/lihtc.html.

EITC caseloads and housing caseloads are number of families, all others are number of individuals.

It is difficult to determine accurately the number of assisted renters, because some are affected by more than one program. Housing caseloads are for 2001. The fraction of households with children depends on housing program. Here it is assumed that half the benefits go to such families.

Medicaid numbers are for 2000 and do not include Hawaii.

Approximately 54 percent of food stamp families have children.

Figures for school nutrition programs include only free and reduced-price meals.

Caseload for CCDBG includes individuals affected by state-only programs.

Notes

Introduction

1. Sheila Zedlewski, Sandra Clark, Eric Meier, Keith and Watson, "Potential Effects of Congressional Welfare Reform Legislation on Family Incomes" Urban Institute, Washington, D.C., July 26, 1996.

2. Barbara Vobejda and Judith Havemann, "Two HHS Officials Quit Over Welfare Changes," *Washington Post*, September 12, 1996, p. A1.

3. Marian Wright Edelman, ". . . Protect Children from Unjust Policies," *Washington Post*, November 3, 1995.

4. Daniel Patrick Moynihan, speech delivered to the U.S. Senate, August 1, 1996; reprinted as "When Principle Is at Issue," in *Washington Post*, August 4, 1996, p. C07.

5. Douglas J. Besharov, "The Past and Future of Welfare Reform," *Public Interest*, (winter 2003).

6. Jason DeParle, *American Dream: Three Women, Ten Kids, and a Nation's Drive to End Welfare* (New York: Viking, 2004).

7. Woodrow Wilson, *Constitutional Government in the United States* (New York: Columbia University Press, 1961), 173.

Chapter 1

1. *Washington Monthly*. "The Mendacity Index: Which President Told the Biggest Whoppers," September 2003.

2. The survey was conducted by the National Opinion Research Center in 1984 and is cited in David Ellwood, *Poor Support* (New York: Basic, 1988).

3. Moffitt, Robert. "Incentive Effects of the U.S. Welfare System: A Review," *Journal of Economic Literature*, 30 (March 1992): 1–61.

4. U.S. House of Representatives, Committee on Ways and Means, *1992 Greenbook* (Washington, D.C.: U.S. Government Printing Office), 590.

5. Craig Gunderson and James Ziliak. "Poverty and Macroeconomic Performance Across Space, Race, and Family Structure," *Demography* 41, no. 1 (February 2004): 61–86.

6. In practice, women were allowed to "disregard" certain expenses before their earnings were docked, and so benefits were reduced by less than one dollar for every dollar earned. Thomas Fraker, Robert Moffitt, and Douglas Wolf ("Effective Tax Rates and Guarantees in the AFDC Program, 1967–1982," *Journal of Human Resources* 20, no. 2 (spring 1985): 251–63) find that effective tax rates were around 70 percent. Perhaps surprisingly, the estimated effects of welfare on labor supply prior to welfare reform had been small. See, for example, Robert Moffitt and Michael Keane, "A Structural Model of Multiple Welfare Program Participation and Labor Supply," *International Economic Review* 39, no. 3 (August 1998): 553–89. They estimate a structural model of participation in multiple welfare programs, and concluded that high welfare "tax" rates had relatively little effect on work effort. See also, Robert Moffitt, "Incentive Effects of the U.S. Welfare System," *Journal of Economic Literature* 30 (1992): 1–61.

7. Kathryn Edin and Laura Lein, *Making Ends Meet: How Single Mothers Survive Welfare and Low-Wage Work* (New York: Russell Sage Foundation, 1997); Rebecca Blank and Patricia Ruggles, "When Do Women use AFDC and Food Stamps?" *Journal of Human Resources* 24, no. 1 (winter 1989): 54–87.

8. Susan Mayer argues in her book *What Money Can't Buy: Family Income and Children's Life Chances* (Cambridge: Harvard University Press, 1997) that there is little evidence that income per se improves outcomes. In their book, *Consequences of Growing Up Poor* (New York: Russell Sage Foundation, 1997), Greg Duncan, Jeanne Brooks-Gunn, and Pamela Klebanov argue that income in the first few years of life is important.

9. Janet Currie and Nancy Cole, "The Link Between AFDC Participation and Birth Weight," *American Economic Review* 283, no. 3 (1993).

10. Phillip Levine and David Zimmerman, "Children's Welfare Exposure and Subsequent Development," NBER Working Paper no. 7522, Cambridge, Mass., February 2000. The authors use data from the National Longitudinal Survey of Youth and examine PIAT mathematics and reading scores, as well as the PPVT and the Behavior Problems Index. In a study using the same data, Anne Hill and June O'Neill argue that welfare had negative effects, but the appendix to their paper shows that when differences between the mothers are controlled for, there are no welfare

effects; see their paper "Family Endowments and the Achievement of Young Children with Special Reference to the Underclass," *Journal of Human Resources* 29, no. 4 (1994): 1064–100.

11. Charles Murray, *Losing Ground* (New York: Basic, 1984); Robert Rector and Patrick Fagan, "How Welfare Harms Kids," Heritage Foundation Backgrounder no. 1084, Washington, D.C., June 1996; Peter Gottschalk, "AFDC Participation Across Generations," *American Economic Review* 80, no. 2 (May 1990): 367–71.

12. David Zimmerman and Phillip Levine, "The Intergenerational Correlation in AFDC Participation: Welfare Trap or Poverty Trap?" Institute for Research on Poverty Discussion Paper no. 1100–96, University of Wisconsin, July 1996.

13. David Ellwood and Mary Joe Bane, "The Impact of AFDC on Family Structure and Living Arrangements," *Research in Labor Economics* 7 (1986); Jonathan Gruber, "Cash Welfare as a Consumption Smoothing Mechanism for Divorced Mothers," *Journal of Public Economics* 75 (2000): 157–82.

14. PRWORA also made legal immigrants ineligble for TANF for their first five years in the country and, as discussed in chapter 5, consolidated some childcare funding programs.

15. For AFDC/TANF caseloads, see U.S. House of Representatives, Committee on Ways and Means, *2004 Green Book*, doc. no. 13-35-13-41 (Washington, D.C.: U.S. Government Printing Office, 2004). See also Jeffrey Grogger, Lynn Karoly, and Jacob Klerman, *Consequences of Welfare Reform: A Research Synthesis* (Santa Monica, Calif.: RAND, 2002).

16. "Primary work activities" included paid or unpaid work, vocational training, job search, and providing child care for other participants. Those subject to work requirements were required to participate in such activities for the first twenty hours of their work requirement. Other types of education or training were allowable after the first twenty hours of work requirements were satisfied. See LaDonna Pavetti, "The Challenge of Achieving High Work Paritcipation Rates in Welfare Programs," Welfare Reform and Beyond Policy Brief no. 31, Brookings Institution, Washington D.C., October 2004.

17. One could have a lengthy debate about whether carrots or sticks are more important. It is likely that many women who were initially kicked off of welfare did not even know about the EITC until they started working. The income supplement may have been instrumental, however, in helping them to stay off welfare.

18. Rebecca Blank, *It Takes a Nation: A New Agenda for Fighting Poverty* (Princeton: Princeton University Press, 1997); Thomas Gais, Richard Nathan, Irene Luire, and Thomas Kaplan, "Implementation of the Personal Responsibility Act of 1996," in *The New World of Welfare: An Agenda for Reauthorization and Beyond* ed. Rebecca Blank and Ron Haskins (Washington, D.C.: Brookings Institution, 2001).

19. Jeffrey Grogger and Charles Michaelopoulos, "Welfare Dynamics Under Time Limits," *Journal of Political Economy* (April 2003). For a discussion of how welfare reform changed welfare offices, see Rebecca Blank, "Evaluating Welfare Reform in the United States," NBER Working Paper no. 8983, Cambridge, Mass., 2002.

20. For an overview of the effects of welfare reform, see National Research Council and Institute of Medicine, *Working Families and Growing Kids: Caring for Children and Adolescents*, ed. Eugene Smolensky and Jennifer Appleton, (Washington, D.C.: National Academies Press, 2003), chapter 7.

21. Wendell Primus, Lynette Rawlings, Kathy Larin, and Kathryn Porter, "The Initial Impacts of Welfare Reform on the Incomes of Single-Mother Families," Center on Budget and Policy Priorities, Washington, D.C. August 22, 1999; Marianne Bitler, Jonah Gelbach, Hilary Hoynes, "What Mean Impacts Miss: Distributional Effects of Welfare Reform Experiments," NBER Working Paper no. 10121, Cambridge, Mass., November, 2003; Jason DeParle, *American Dream: Three Women, Ten Kids, and a Nation's Drive to End Welfare* (New York: Viking, 2004).

22. National Research Council and Institute for Medicine, *Working Families and Growing Kids*, p. 219; Jason DeParle quoted in "Whither Welfare Reform? Lessons from the Wisconsin Experience," Manhattan Institute, New York, September 21, 2004.

23. Jeffrey Grogger, Lynn Karoly, and Jacob Klerman, *Consequences of Welfare Reform: A Research Synthesis* (Santa Monica, Calif.: RAND, 2002); Pamela Morris, V. Know, and Lisa Gennetian, "Welfare Policies Matter for Children and Youth: Lessons for TANF Reauthorization," Manpower Demonstration Research Corporation, available at http://www.mdrc.org/Reports2002/NG_PolicyBrief/NG_PolicyBrief.htm[2002]; Martha Zaslow, Kristin Moore, J. L. Brooks, K. Toot, Z. A. Redd, and C. A. Emig, "Experimental Studies of Weflare Reform and Children," *Future of Children* 23 (2002): 79–98.

24. For a summary of this literature see Janet Currie, "When Do We Really Know What We Think We Know? Determining Causality," in

Work, Family, Health and Well-Being, ed. Suzanne Bianchi and Lynn Casper. (Mahwah, N.J.: Lawrence Earlbaum, 2004).

25. James Ziliak, "Filling the Poverty Gap, Then and Now," online discussion paper, University of Kentucky Center for Poverty Research, 2004.

26. Mark Duggan and Melissa Kearney, "The Rise in SSI Participation among Children: Assessing the Impact on Poverty and Labor Supply," paper presented at the NBER Summer Institute, Cambridge, Mass., August 2004. Among children, SSI participation rose dramatically following a 1990 Supreme Court ruling (*Sullivan v. Zebley*) that allowed children to be eligible on the basis of individual assessments. In 1996, PRWORA eliminated these assessments and allowed only children whose disability was on a specified list to receive SSI. In addition, children with "maladaptive behaviors" were eliminated from the list.

27. The story of Laura and Simon is fictional, but based on a real family I know.

28. All of the numbers in this example are based on 2003 values. For details, see U.S. House of Representatives Committee on Ways and Means, *2004 Green Book.*

29. Nada Eissa and Jeffrey Liebman, "Labor Supply Response to the Earned Income Tax Credit," *Quarterly Journal of Economics* 112, no. 2 (May 1996): 605–37; Bruce Meyer and Daniel Rosenbaum, "Welfare, the Earned Income Tax Credit, and the Labor Supply of Single Mothers," *Quarterly Journal of Economics* 116, no. 3 (August 2001): 1063–115.

30. Jeffrey Grogger, "Welfare Transitions in the 1990s: The Economy, Welfare Policy, and the EITC," NBER Working Paper no. 9472, Cambridge, Mass., February 2003.

31. J. Romich and T. Weisner, "How Families View and Use the EITC: Advance Payment versus Lump Sum Delivery," *National Tax Journal* 53 (2000): 1245–64.

32. Wojciech Kopczuk and Cristian Popl-Eleches, "Electronic Filing, Tax Preparers, and Participation in the Earned Income Tax Credit," Manuscript Department of Economics, Columbia University, June 2, 2004; John Karl Scholz. "The Earned Income Tax Credit: Participation, Compliance, and Anti-Poverty Effectiveness" *National Tax Journal* (March 1994): 59–81.

33. See Robert Greenstein, "Welfare Reform's Hidden Ally," *American Prospect*, July 15, 2002; and Janet McCubbin. "EITC Noncompliance: The Determinants of the Misreporting of Children," *National Tax Journal* 53, no. 2 (2000): 1135–64.

34. There is overwhelming evidence that one reason that single parent-hood is bad for children is that single parents are more likely to be poor. Marriage is a route out of poverty for many single women, but the evidence suggests that stepfathers (and stepmothers) are not as good for children as biological parents (on average). See Sara McLanahan and Gary Sandefur, *Growing Up with a Single Parent* (Cambridge: Harvard University Press, 1994); and Anne Case, I-Fen Lin, and Sara McLanahan, "How Hungry is the Selfish Gene," *Economic Journal* 110, no. 466 (October 2000): 781–805. For an example of a study that examines the growth in welfare-to-work women's earnings over time, see David Card and Dean Hyslop, "Estimating the Dynamic Treatment Effects of an Earnings Subsidy for Welfare Leavers," *Industrial and Labor Relations Review* (forthcoming), which, as one of the best studies to date, finds little evidence of growth. Other studies find some growth, but not enough to greatly change the economic situation of these low-income households. See Sheldon Danziger, Colleen Heflin, Mary Corcoran, Elizabeth Oltmans, and Hui-Chen Wang, "Does It Pay to Move from Welfare to Work?" *Journal of Policy Analysis and Management* 21, no. 4 (fall 2002): 671–92; and Susanna Loeb and Mary Corcoran, "Welfare, Work Experience and Economic Self-Sufficiency," *Journal of Policy Analysis and Management* 20, no. 1 (winter 2001): 1–20.

35. Another possibility is that immigration has depressed wages at the bottom of the income distribution. There is, however, remarkably little evidence that immigration has much effect on the wages of native-born workers. Instead, immigrants appear to compete most closely with other immigrants. See Joseph Altonji and David Card, "The Effects of Immigration on the Labor Market Outcomes of Less-Skilled Natives," in *Immigration, Trade, and the Labor Market*, ed. John Abowd and Richard Freeman (Chicago: University of Chicago Press, 1991), 407–21; David Card, "The Impact of the Mariel Boatlift on the Miami Labor Market," *Industrial and Labor Relations Review* (January 1990); George Borjas. "The Economic Analysis of Immigration," in *The Handbook of Labor Economics*, ed. David Card and Orley Ashenfelter, volume 3a (New York: North Holland, 1999), chapter 28.

36. Saul Hoffman and Laurence Seidman, *Helping Working Families: The Earned Income Tax Credit* (Kalamazoo, Mich.: Upjohn Institute for Employment Research, 2002). In his doctoral dissertation, Andrew Leigh finds that a 10 percent increase in the generosity of the EITC is associated with a 4 percent fall in the wages of high school dropouts. He does not,

however, distinguish between male or female workers or directly link these changes in wages to the changes in labor supply among the different groups. Also, he finds that the EITC has a larger negative effect on wages in states with high minimum wages, which is counterintuitive (see the discussion of minimum wages later in this book; see Andrew Leigh, "Essays in Poverty and Inequality," Ph.D. diss., Harvard University, May 2004).

37. The Carter plan was called "Program for Better Jobs and Income" and covered childless couples and singles as well as families with children. The Nixon plan was called the "Family Assistance Plan."

38. The Avrin and the Pozdena and Johnson papers are in Philip K. Robins, ed., *A Guaranteed Annual Income: Evidence from a Social Experiment* (New York: Academic, 1980). The Mallar, Poirier, and Wooldridge papers come from Harold Watts and Albert Rees, eds. *The New Jersey Income Maintenance Experiments* (New York: Academic, 1977). The O'Conner et al. and the Maynard and Crawford studies appear in *Rural Income Maintenance Experiment: Final Report*, (Madison, Wis.: Institute for Research on Poverty, 1976). The other NIT studies referred to this section are Rebecca Maynard and Richard Murnane, "The Effects of Negative Income Tax on School Performance: Results of an Experiment," *Journal of Human Resources* 14, no. 4 (1979); Steven Venti. "The Effects of Income Maintenance on Work, Schooling, and Non-Market Activities of Youth," *Review of Economics and Statistics* 66, no. 1 (February 1984): 16–25.

39. See Robert Michael, "The Consumption Experiments," in *Welfare in Rural Areas*, ed. J. L. Palmer and J. A. Pechman (Washington, D.C.: Brookings Institution, 1978); Lisa Barrow and Leslie McGranahan, "The EITC and Durable Goods Purchases," *National Tax Journal* 53, no. 4, part 2 (December 2000): 1211–44.

40. Timothy Smeeding, Katherin Ross Phillips, and Michael O'Connor, "The EITC: Expectation, Knowledge, Use, and Economic and Social Mobility," *National Tax Journal* 53, no. 4 (December 2000): 1187–209.

41. David Card and Alan Krueger *Myth and Measurement* (Princeton: Princeton University Press, 1997).

42. See David Card. "Do Minimum Wages Reduce Employment? A Case Study of California, 1987–89," *Industrial and Labor Relations Review* 4, no. 1 (October 1992): 38–54.

43. One commentator on this book argues that the real problem with a baby bonus is that it is a "return to an entitlement" and thus would have all the problems of AFDC. I disagree. I have been at some pains to

describe the ways in which AFDC rules discouraged work and marriage. A universal baby bonus would not have these effects.

Chapter 2

1. This is a true story, though names have been changed.

2. Adam Atherly, Seymore Williams, and Stephen Reed, "The Cost of Asthma to Employers," Centers for Disease Control Washington, D.C., 1999. This study used 1997 claims data from the Medstat database.

3. Figures in this paragraph are from Emily Cornell, "MCH Update 2002: State Health Coverage for Low-Income Pregnant Women, Children and Parents," National Governor's Association Center for Best Practices, Washington, D.C., June 9, 2003. Technically, the cutoff in Vermont and Connecticut was 300 percent of the federal poverty line.

4. See Janet Currie and Duncan Thomas, "Medical Care for Children: Public Insurance, Private Insurance and Racial Differences in Utilization," *Journal of Human Resources* 30, no. 1 (winter 1995): 135–62; Mary D. Overpeck and Jonathan Kotch, "The Effect of US Children's Access to Care on Medical Attention for Injuries," *American Journal of Public Health* 85, no. 3 (March 1995): 402–4; Michael Kogan et al., "The Effect of Gaps in Health Insurance on Continuity of a Regular Source of Care among Preschool-Aged Children in the United States," *Journal of the American Medical Association* 274, no. 18 (November 8, 1995): 1429–35; Children's Defense Fund, "14 Things You Should Know about the New Child Health Program," Washington, D.C., September 4, 1997.

5. See Joseph P. Newhouse, *Free for All? Lessons from the RAND Health Insurance Experiment* (Cambridge: Harvard University Press, 1993).

6. Abigail Trafford, "A Different Kind of Spin," *Washington Post*, October 7, 2003, p. F01; Shailesh Bhandari and Elizabeth Gifford. "Children with Health Insurance: 2001," Current Population Reports P60-224, U.S. Census Bureau, Washington, D.C., August 2003.

7. For more details about Medicaid, see the U.S. House of Representatives, Committee on Ways and Means, *2004 Green Book*, 108–6; and Centers for Medicare and Medicaid Services, "Program Information on Medicare, Medicaid, SCHIP, and Other Programs of the Centers for Medicare and Medicaid Services," CMS Office of Research Development and Information, Washington, D.C., June 2002. See also http://www.whitehouse.gov/omb/budget/fy2002/guide02.html.

8. In some states, children could also qualify for Medicaid under state "Medically Needy" programs or "Ribicoff" programs. The Medically Needy program relaxed the income criteria for eligibility by covering people whose large medical expenditures brought their incomes below some specified threshold. Medically Needy thresholds were above AFDC thresholds, but they were never more than 33 percent higher. The Ribicoff option allowed states to use federal matching money to cover some categories of children in two-parent families that met the AFDC income criteria. Relatively few children, however, were covered under these programs.

9. The material in this section is drawn from Janet Currie and Jonathan Gruber, "Saving Babies: The Efficacy and Cost of Recent Changes in the Medicaid Eligibility of Pregnant Women," *Journal of Political Economy* 104, no. 6 (December 1996): 1263–46; and Currie and Gruber, "Health Insurance Eligibility, Utilization of Medical Care, and Child Health," *Quarterly Journal of Economics* 111, no. 2 (May 1996): 431–66.

10. Associated Press, "CHIP Extends to 1.2 Million Kids, 8 States," April 1, 1998.

11. See National Governor's Association (NGA), "State Strategies for Increasing Health Care Coverage for Children," Washington, D.C., March 4, 1997; NGA, "New State Efforts to Provide Health Care Coverage for Uninsured Children," Washington, D.C., April 22, 1997; NGA, "Providing Health Insurance Coverage to Uninsured Children," Washington, D.C., May 1, 1995.

12. This index is constructed by taking a national sample of women (or children) and asking what fraction of this fixed sample would be eligible for Medicaid under the rules in effect in each state and year (Currie and Gruber, "Saving Babies" and "Health Insurance Eligibility"). These figures refer to children less than fifteen only. We focused on children one to fourteen years old because pregnant teens could be eligible for Medicaid coverage of pregnancy, and we wished to focus on the expansions for children.

13. Children's Defense Fund, "14 Things You Should Know."

14. Anna Aizer, "Low Take-Up in Medicaid: Does Outreach Matter and For Whom?" *American Economic Review* 93, no. 2 (May 2003): 238–41; Anna Aizer and Janet Currie, "The Impact of Outreach on Medi-Cal Enrollment and Child Health: Lessons from California," final report prepared for California Policy Research Center, University of California, California Program on Access to Care, September 30, 2002.

15. Leemore Dafny and Jonathan Gruber, "Does Public Insurance Improve the Efficiency of Medical Care? Medicaid Expansions and Child Hospitalizations," NBER Working Paper no. 7555, Cambridge, Mass., February 2000.

16. Susan Brink, "The Smallest Preemie," *U.S. News and World Reports*, March 30, 1998, pp. 60–69; D'Angio, C. T., R. A. Sinkin, T. P. Stevens, N. K. Landfish, J. L Merzbach, R. M. Ryan, D. L. Phelps, D. R. Palumbo, and G. J. Myers. "Longitudinal, 15-year Follow-up of Children Born at Less than 29 Weeks' Gestation after Introduction of Surfactant Therapy into a Region: Nerologic, Cognitive, and Educational Outcomes," *Pediatrics* 110, no. 6 (December 2002): 1094–102.

17. Actually, only hospitals that treat Medicare patients are specifically prohibited from turning away women in labor, but this includes most hospitals. See Saywell et al., "Hospital and Patient Characteristics of Uncompensated Hospital Care: Policy Implications," *Journal of Health Politics, Policy, and Law* 14 (1989): 287–307; U.S. General Accounting Office, "Health Care Reform: Potential Difficulties in Determining Eligibility for Low-Income People," no. GAO/HEHS-94-176, Washington, D.C., July 1994.

18. National Governor's Association, "Promising Practices to Improve Results for Young Children," August 30, 1997; see www.nga.org.

19. U.S. Census Bureau, "Health Insurance Coverage in the United States: 2000," Washington, D.C., September 2003; Children's Defense Fund, "14 Things You Should Know"; David Card and Lara Shore-Sheppard, "Using Discontinuous Eligibility Rules to Identify the Effects of the Federal Medicaid Expansions on Low Income Children," *Review of Economics and Statistics* 86, no. 3 (2004): 752–66.

20. Much of the discussion in this section is drawn from U.S. General Accounting Office, "Health Care Reform."

21. Janet Currie, "Do Children of Immigrants Make Differential Use of Public Health Insurance?," *Issues in the Economics of Immigration*, George Borjas (ed.), Chicago: University of Chicago Press for NBER, 2000, 271–308. Ruth E. Zambrana et al., "The Relationship Between Psychosocial Status of Immigrant Latino Mothers and Use of Emergency Pediatric Services," *Health and Social Work* 19, no. 2 (May 1994): 93–102.

22. David Himmelstein, Elizabeth Warren, Deborah Thorne, and Steffie Woolhandler, "MarketWatch: Illness and Injury as Contributors to Bankruptcy," *Health Affairs* (February 2005). Their data indicates that 28 percent of survey respondents identified medical bills as a contributing factor in their bankruptcies.

23. See U.S. General Accounting Office, "Health Care Reform."

24. Ibid.

25. Alissa Rubin, "Poor Children Falling Out of Medicaid's Safety Net," *Los Angeles Times*, November 18, 1997, p. A1.

26. Cynthia Bansak and Steven Raphael, "The Effects of State Policy Design Features on Take-Up and Crowd-Out Rates for the State Children's Health Insurance Program," Goldman School of Public Policy, University of California, Berkeley, November 2004.

27. Beth K. Yudkowsky, Jennifer Cartland, and Samuel Flint, "Pediatrician Participation in Medicaid: 1978 to 1989," *Pediatrics* 85, no. 4 (April 1990): 567–77.

28. Robert F. St. Peter, Paul Newacheck, and Neal Halfon, "Access to Care for Poor Children: Separate and Unequal?" *Journal of the American Medical Association* 267, no. 20 (May 27, 1992): 2760–764; Sandra Decker, "The Effect of Physician Reimbursement Levels on the Primary Care of Medicaid Patients," working paper, New York University Graduate School of Public Service, November 1992.

29. Josh Barbanel, "Newborn Fatalities High at New York Hospitals," *New York Times*, June 9, 1995; Henry Waxman, "Kids and Medicaid: Progress but Continuing Problems," *American Journal of Public Health* 79 (1989): 1217–18.

30. These comments are from a survey conducted by the Alan Guttmacher Institute (New York) in 1986: "The Financing of Maternity Care in the United States," published in 1988. See also Physician Payment Review Commission, "Physician Payment Under Medicaid," Washington, D.C., 1991.

31. Janet B. Mitchell and Rachel Schurman, "Access to Private Obstetrics/Gynecology Services Under Medicaid," *Medical Care* 22, no. 11 (November 1984): 1026–37.

32. Anne L. Reisinger, David Colby, and Anne Schwartz, "Medicaid Physician Payment Reform: Using the Medicare Fee Schedule for Medicaid Payments," *American Journal of Public Health* 84, no. 4 (April 1994): 553–60.

33. Carol C. Korenbrot et al., "Professional Liability Reform and Access to Medicaid Obstetric Care in New York State," *New York State Journal of Medicine* 92, no. 6 (June 1992): 237–45.

34. Diane Rowland and Alina Salganicoff, "Commentary: Lessons from Medicaid—Improving Access to Office-Based Physician Care for the Low-Income Population," *Public Health Policy Forum* 84, no. 4 (April 1994): 550–52.

35. See, for example, Jack Hadley, "Physician Participation in Medicaid: Evidence from California," *Health Services Research* 4 (1979): 266–80; John Holahan, "Medicaid Physician Fees, 1990: The Results of a New Survey," report no. 6110-01 Urban Institute, Washington, D.C., October 1991; and Stephen H. Long, Russle Settle, and Bruce Stuart, "Reimbursement and Access to Physician's Services Under Medicaid," *Journal of Health Economics* 5, no. 3 (1986): 235–51. Baker and Royalty, however, find much weaker effects in a study that examines the same physicians over time and focuses on the effects of a 1989 federal requirement that states increase fees for obstetric care to levels sufficient to ensure the availability of physician services. See Laurence Baker and Anne Royalty, "Medicaid Policy, Physician Behavior, and Health Care for the Low-Income Population," manuscript, Department of Economics Stanford University, December 1996.

36. Carol C. Korenbrot et al. "Evaluation of California's Statewide Implementation of Enhanced Perinatal Services as Medicaid Benefits," *Public Health Reports* 110, no. 2 (March–April, 1995): 125–33; Decker, "The Effect of Physician Reimbursement Levels," Janet Currie, Jonathan Gruber, and Michael Fischer, "Physician Payments and Infant Mortality: Evidence From Medicaid Fee Policy," *American Economic Review* 85, no. 2 (May 1995): 106–11; Joel W. Cohen, "Medicaid Policy and the Substitution of Hospital Outpatient Care for Physician Care," *Health Services Research* 24, no. 1 (April 1989): 34–66.

37. Testimony before the U.S. Senate, Committee on Finance, on "Health Care Coverage for Children," June 29, 1989.

38. Janet Currie and Jonathan Gruber, "The Technology of Birth: Health Insurance, Medical Interventions, and Infant Health," NBER Working Paper no. 5985, Cambridge, Mass., 1997.

39. James Fries, C. Everett Koop, et al. "Beyond Health Promotion: Reducing Need and Demand for Medical Care," *Health Affairs* 17, no. 2 (1998): 70–83.

40. See Jennifer S. Hass, Seven Udarhelyi, and Arnold Epstein, "The Effect of Health Coverage for Uninsured Pregnant Women on Maternal Health and the Use of Cesarean Section," *Journal of the American Medical Association* 270, no. 20 (July 1993): 61–64.

41. David Cutler, *Your Money or Your Life: Strong Medicine for America's Health Care System* (London: Oxford University Press, 2004).

42. Rebecca Blank and Patricia Ruggles, "When Do Women Use AFDC and Food Stamps? The Dynamics of Eligibility vs. Participation," *The Journal of Human Resources* 31, no. 1 (winter 1996): 57–89.

43. Lara Shore-Sheppard, "Stemming the Tide? The Effect of Expanding Medicaid Eligibility on Health Insurance Coverage?" manuscript, Department of Economics, University of Pittsburgh, November 1997.

44. See David Cutler and Jonathan Gruber, "Does Public Insurance Crowd Out Public Insurance?" *The Quarterly Journal of Economics* 111, no. 2 (May 1996): 391–430.

45. Lisa Dubay and Genevieve Kenney, "Did Medicaid Expansions for Pregnant Women Crowd Out Private Coverage?" *Health Affairs* 16, no. 1 (January/February 1997): 185–93.

46. U.S. House of Representatives, Committee on Ways and Means, *2004 Green Book*.

47. Diane Rowland et al., *Medicaid and Managed Care: Lessons from the Literature* (Washington, D.C.: Henry J. Kaiser Family Foundation, 1995).

48. U.S. General Accounting Office, "Medicaid: Oversight of Health Maintenance Organizations in the Chicago Area," GA/HRD 90-81, Washington, D.C., 1990; U.S. General Accounting Office, "Medicaid Managed Care: More Competition and Oversight Would Improve California's Expansion Plan," GAO/HEHS-95-87, Washington, D.C., 1995.

49. Anna Aizer, Janet Currie, and Enrico Moretti. "Competition in Imperfect Markets: Does it Help California's Medicaid Mothers?" NBER Working Paper no. 10430, Cambridge, Mass., April 2004. See also Mark Duggan, "Does Contracting Out Increase the Efficiency of Government Programs? Evidence from Medicaid HMOs," *Journal of Public Economics* 88, no. 12 (2004): 2549–72. Laurence Baker, Susan Schmitt, and Ciaran Phibbs. "Medicaid Managed Care in California and Health Care for Newborns," manuscript, Department of Health Research and Policy, Stanford University, March 2003.

50. Leighton Ku and Sashi Nimalendran, "Losing Out: States Are Cutting 1.2 to 1.6 Million Low-Income People from Medicaid, SCHIP, and Other State Health Insurance Programs," Center on Budget and Policy Priorities, Washington, D.C., December 22, 2003. George Benjamin and Peter Leibig are quoted in Miriam Jordan, "Prenatal Care Is Latest State Cut in Services for Illegal Immigrants," *Wall Street Journal*, October 18, 2004, p. A1.

51. Stephanie Simon, "States Rein in Health Costs," *Los Angeles Times*, April 14, 2005, p. A1.

52. Thomas MaCurdy, "Medi-Cal Expenditures: Long-Term Forecasts and Policy Challenges," xerox, Stanford University Department of Economics, April 2005.

Chapter 3

1. For more information about these programs see "Food and Nutrition Service Program Data," at fns1.usda.gov/fns/MENU/ABOUT/PRO-GRAMS/PROGDATA.HTM. For a discussion of the rationale for the National School Lunch Program, see the *Congressional Record-House*, February 19, 1946, p. 1455. The two reports mentioned are: U.S. Senate, Committee on Labor and Public Welfare, Subcommittee on Employment, Manpower, and Poverty, "Hunger in America; Chronology and Selected Background Materials," Washington, D.C., 1968; and U.S. Senate, Committee on Agriculture, Nutrition and Forestry, Subcommittee on Nutrition, "Hunger in America, ten years later : hearing before the Subcommittee on Nutrition of the Committee on Agriculture, Nutrition, and Forestry," Washington, D.C., April 30, 1979. See also Jean Mayer, "National and International Issues in Food Policy," Lowell Lecture at Harvard University, May 15, 1989; available at http://www.dce.harvard.edu/pubs/lowell/jmayer.html.

2. Mark Nord, Margaret Andrews, and Steven Carlson, "Household Food Security in the United States, 2002," Food Assistance and Nutrition Research Report no. FANRR35, Economic Research Service United States Department of Agriculture, Washington, D.C., October 2003.

3. Jayanta Bhattacharya, Janet Currie, Steven Haider, and Thomas DeLeire, "Heat or Eat? Income Shocks and the Allocation of Nutrition in American Families," *American Journal of Public Health* 93, no. 7 (July 2003): 1149–54.

4. J. Murphy, J. Michael, Cheryl Wehler, Maria Pagano, et al., "Relationship Between Hunger and Psychosocial Functioning in Low-Income American Children," *Journal of the American Academy of Child and Adolescent Psychiatry* 37, no. 2 (1998): 163–70; K. Alaimo, C. M. Olson, E. A. Frongillo, "Food Insufficiency and American School-Aged Children's Cognitive, Academic, and Psychosocial Development," *Pediatrics* 108, no. 1 (July 2001): 44–53.

5. Jason DeParle, quoted in "Whither Welfare Reform: Lessons from the Wisconsin Experience."

6. U.S. Department of Health and Human Services, *The Surgeon General's Call to Action to Prevent and Decrease Overweight and Obesity, 2001* (Rockville, Md.: Office of the Surgeon General, 2001); Jayanta Bhattacharya, Janet Currie, and Steven Haider, "Poverty, Food Insecurity, and Nutritional Outcomes in Children and Adults," *Journal of Health Economics* 23, no. 2 (2004): 839–62; E. Luder, E. Ceysens-Okada, A. Loren-Roth,

et al., "Health and Nutrition Surveys in a Group of Urban Homeless Adults," *Journal of the American Dietetic Association* 90 (1990): 1387–92; W. D. Dietz, "Does Hunger Cause Obesity?" *Pediatrics* 95, no. 5 (1995): 766–67; S. J. Jones, L. Jahns, B. A. Baraia, and B. Haughton, "Lower Risk of Overweight in School-Aged Food-Insecure Girls Who Participate in Food Assistance: Results from the Panel Study of Income Dynamics Child Development Supplement," *Archives of Pediatric and Adolescent Medicine* 157, no. 8 (August 2003): 780–84.

7. See U.S. House of Representatives, Committee on Ways and Means, *Green Book 2004*. This example and much of the discussion in this chapter is from Janet Currie, "U.S. Food and Nutrition Programs," in *Means-Tested Transfer Programs in the United States*, ed. Robert Moffitt (Chicago: University of Chicago Press for NBER, 2003).

8. James C. Ohls, Thomas M. Fraker, A. P. Martini, et al., "Effects of Cash-Out on Food Use by Food Stamp Program Participants in San Diego," Mathematica Policy Research, Princeton, N.J., 1992; Diane Whitmore, "What Are Food Stamps Worth?" Princeton Industrial Relations Section Working Paper no. 468, July 2002; U.S. Department of Agriculture, "The Extent of Trafficking in the Food Stamp Program: 1999–2002," U.S.D.A. Food and Nutrition Service Office of Analysis Nutrition and Evaluation, Washington, D.C., July 2003; Anne Ciemnecki, Lara Hulsey, James Ohls, et al., "Final Report for the Food Stamp Participant Trafficking Study," no. 8171-091, Mathematica Policy Research, Washington, D.C., March 1998.

The trafficking study indicates that rates of fraud have fallen significantly since 1996–98 (when about 4 cents on the dollar was lost). This may be because of the introduction of electronic benefit cards, which are harder to sell and which also make it harder for stores to defraud the government by buying coupons at a discount.

9. The marriage disincentives discussed in chapter 1 mean that it is often in the interest of cohabiting partners not to marry. For evidence regarding the number of female heads who cohabit, see Robert Moffitt, Robert Reville, and Anne Winkler, "Beyond Single Mothers: Cohabitation and Marriage in the AFDC Program," *Demography* 35, no. 3 (August 1998): 259–78.

10. J. S. Butler and J. E. Raymond, "The Effect of the Food Stamp Program on Nutrient Intake," *Economic Inquiry* 34 (1996): 781–98; P. Peter Basiotis, Carol S. Kramer-LeBlanc, and Eileen T. Kennedy, "Maintaining Nutrition Security and Diet Quality: The Role of the Food Stamp

Program and WIC," *Family Economics and Nutrition Review* 11, nos. 1–2 (1998): 4–16.

11. Barbara Cohen, James Ohls, Margaret Andrews, et al., *Food Stamp Participants' Food Security and Nutrient Availability, Final Report*, contract no. 53-3198-4-025, Food and Nutrition Service, U.S. Department of Agriculture, Washington, D.C., July 1999; Jayanta Bhattacharya and Janet Currie, "Youths at Nutritional Risk: Malnourished or Misnourished?" in *Youths at Risk*, ed. Jonathan Gruber (Chicago: University of Chicago Press for NBER, 2000).

12. For a detailed summary of these studies see "U.S. Food and Nutrition Programs," in *Means-Tested Transfer Programs in the United States*, ed. R. Moffitt.

13. Barbara Devaney and Robert Moffitt, "Dietary Effects of the Food Stamp Program," *American Journal of Agricultural Economics* 73, no. 1 (1991): 202–11; J. T. Cook, L. P. Sherman, and J. L. Brown, "Impact of Food Stamps on the Dietary Adequacy of Poor Children," Center on Hunger Poverty and Nutrition Policy, Tufts School of Nutrition, Medford, Mass., 1995; D. C. Rose, D. Smallwood, and J. Blaylock, "Socioeconomic Factors Associated with the Iron Intake of Preschoolers in the United States," *Nutrition Research*, 15, no. 9 (1995): 1297–309.

14. Basiotis, Kramer-LeBlanc, and Kennedy, "Maintaining Nutrition Security and Diet Quality"; Bhattacharya and Currie, "Youths at Nutritional Risk"; D. C. Rose, C. Gunderson, and V. Oliveira, "Determinants of Food Insecurity in the United States. Evidence from the SIPP and CS-FII Datasets," Technical Bulletin no. 1869, U.S. Department of Agriculture, Washington, D.C., 1998.

15. Michael Ponza, James Ohls, Lorenzo Moreno, et al., "Customer Service in the Food Stamp Program," contract no. 53-3198-40-025, Food and Nutrition Service, U.S. Department of Agriculture, Washington, D.C., July 1999.

16. Doug O'Brien, Kimberly Prendergast, Eleanor Thompson, Marcus Fruchter, and Halley Torres Aldeen, "The Red Tape Divide: State-by-State Review of Food Stamp Applications," *American's Second Harvest* (August, 2000); Nina Bernstein, "Bingo, Blood and Burial Plots in the Quest for Food Stamps," *New York Times*, August 12, 2000, p. A1.

17. Janet Currie and Jeffrey Grogger, "Explaining Recent Declines in Food Stamp Program Participation," in *Brookings Papers on Urban Affairs*, edited by William Gale and Janet Rothenberg-Pack (Washington, D.C.: Brookings Institution, 2001), 203–244.

18. Beth Daponte, Seth Sanders, and Lowell Taylor, "Why Do Low-Income Households Not Use Food Stamps? Evidence from an Experiment," *Journal of Human Resources* 34, no. 3 (summer 1999): 612–28. Rebecca Blank and Patricia Ruggles provide additional evidence that take-up varies with benefit amounts, in their paper "When Do Women Use AFDC and Food Stamps? The Dynamics of Eligibility vs. Participation," *Journal of Human Resources* 31, no. 1 (winter 1996): 57–89.

19. Aaron Yelowitz. "Did Recent Medicaid Reforms Cause the Caseload Explosion in the Food Stamps Program?" Institute for Research on Poverty Working Paper no. 1109–96, September 1996.

20. U.S. House of Representatives, Committee on Ways and Means, *1998 Green Book* (Washington, D.C.: U.S. Government Printing Office) 1998; Sheila Zedlewski and Sarah Brauner, "Declines in Food Stamp and Welfare Participation: Is There a Connection?" Urban Institute, Washington, D.C., 1999; M. Robin Dion and LaDonna Pavetti, "Access and Participation in Medicaid and the Food Stamp Program: A Review of the Recent Literature," Mathematica Policy Research, Washington, D.C., March 2000; Parke Wilde, "The Decline in Food Stamp Participation in the 1990s" USDA Food and Nutrition Research Program, Washington D.C., June 2000. Some categories of persons, such as resident aliens and adults without dependents who do not meet work requirements, have become ineligible as a result of PWRORA. Since these groups did not make up much of the FSP caseload before PWRORA, however, it is unlikely that their exclusion is responsible for much of the decline in caseloads.

21. California State Auditor, "Statewide Fingerprint Imaging System: The State Must Weigh Factors Other Than Need and Cost-Effectiveness When Determining Future Funding for the System," no. 2001–015, Bureau of State Audits Sacramento, Calif., January 2003.

22. Keri Sender et al., "Stamping Out Hunger: Access to Food Stamp Applications in New York City," a report to the New York City Council, September 2003.

23. Estimates of the size of this effect are small, however. See Robert Moffitt and Thomas Fraker, "The Effect of Food Stamps on Labor Supply: A Bivariate Selection Model," *Journal of Public Economics* 35, no. 1 (February 1988): 25–56.

24. Most of the following information about the WIC program comes from these sources: Marianne Bitler, Janet Currie, and John Karl Scholz, "WIC Eligibility and Participation," *Journal of Human Resources* 38 (2003): 1139–79; U.S. Congress, *Consolidated Federal Regulations*, 1-1-96 ed.

(Washington, D.C.: U.S. Government Printing Office, 1996); Bonnie Randall, Lyria Boast, and Laurin Holst, "Study of WIC Participant and Program Characteristics, 1994," FNS 53-3198-9-002, Office of Analyses and Evaluation, Food and Consumer Service, Washington, D.C., December 1995; U.S. House of Representatives, Committee on Ways and Means, *1999 Green Book* (Washington, D.C.: U.S. Government Printing Office, 1999); W. L. Hamilton, Mary K. Fox, et al., "Nutrition and Health Outcomes Study: Review of the Literature, 2nd draft, Abt Associates, Cambridge, Mass., 2000. Other sources are noted, where appropriate.

25. Douglas J. Besharov and Peter Germanis, *Rethinking WIC: An Evaluation of the Women, Infants and Children Program* (Washington, D.C.: AEI Press, 2001). See Bitler, Currie, and Scholz, "WIC Eligibility and Participation."

26. National Research Council Committee on National Statistics, *Estimating Eligibility and Participation for the WIC Program: Phase I Report*, ed. Michelle Ver Ploeg and David Betson (Washington, D.C.: National Academy Press, 2001).

27. U.S. General Accounting Office, "Federal Investments Like WIC Can Produce Savings, GAO/HRD9218, Washington, D.C., 1992.

28. Mayer, "National and International Issues in Food Policy."

29. Besharov and Rossi, *Rethinking WIC*.

30. Later studies include I. B. Ahluwalia, V. K. Hogan, L. Grummer-strawn, et al., "The Effect of WIC Participation on Small-for-Gestational-Age Births," *American Journal of Public Health* 88, no. 9 (1992): 1374–77; H. L. Brown, K. Watkins, and H. K. Hiett, "The Impact of the Women, Infants, and Children Food Supplemental Program on Birth Outcome," *American Journal of Obstetrics and Gynecology* 174 (1996): 1279–83; A. Gordon and L. Nelson, "Characteristics and Outcomes of WIC Participants and Nonparticipants: Analysis of the 1988 National Maternal and Infant Health Survey," Food and Nutrition Service, U.S. Department of Agriculture, Alexandria, Va. 1995; Barbara Devaney, "Very Low Birthweight Among Medicaid Newborns in Five States: The Effects of Prenatal WIC Participation," Food and Nutrition Service, U.S. Department of Agriculture, Alexandria, Va. 1992; Lori Kowaleski-Jones and Greg Duncan, "Effects of Participation in the WIC Program on Birthweight: Evidence from the National Longitudinal Survey of Youth," *American Journal of Public Health* 92, no. 5 (2002): 799–804; Janet Currie and Marianne Bitler, "Does WIC Work? The Effect of WIC on Pregnancy and Birth Outcomes," *Journal of Policy Analysis and Management* 23, no. 4 (fall 2004); Nancy

Burstein, Mary Kay Fox, Jordan B. Hiller, Robert Kornfeld, et al., "WIC General Analysis Project, Profile of WIC Children," ABT Associates, Cambridge, Mass., March 2000.

A recent study questions the consensus on WIC. See Theodore Joyce, Diane Gibson, and Silvie Colman, "The Changing Association Between Prenatal Participation in WIC and Birth Outcomes in New York City," *Journal of Policy Analysis and Management*, forthcoming. In our comment on their work, Marianne Bitler and I point out that their estimates are not actually very different from those in the literature. Joyce et al. argue, however, that it is impossible for WIC to affect preterm birth, and so the estimated positive effects of WIC on preterm birth prove that all the estimated positive effects of WIC are statistical artifacts of some sort. We take issue with this interpretation. See Janet Currie and Marianne Bitler, "The Changing Association Between Prenatal Participation in WIC and Birth Outcomes in New York City: What Does it Mean?" *Journal of Policy Analysis and Management*, 2005.

31. See the review in Janet Currie, "U.S. Food and Nutrition Programs," in *Means-Tested Transfer Programs in the United States*, ed. R. Moffitt.

32. Victor Olviera and Mark Prell, "Sharing the Economic Burden: Who Pays for WIC's Infant Formula?" USDA Economic Research Service, September 2004.

33. Nancy Burstein, Mary Kay Fox, and Michael J. Puma, *Study of the Impact of WIC on the Growth and Development of Children: Field Test. Volume II: Preliminary Impact Estimates* (Cambridge, Mass. Abt Associates, 1991); Pinka Chatterji and Jeanne Brooks-Gunn, "WIC Participation, Breast-feeding Practices and Well-Baby Care among Unmarried, Low-Income Mothers," *American Journal of Public Health*, 2004.

34. D. C. Rose, J. P. Habicht, and B. Devaney, "Household Participation in the Food Stamp and WIC Programs Increases the Nutrient Intakes of Preschool Children," *Journal of Nutrition* 128 (1998); 548–55; R. Yip, N. Binkin, L. Fleshood, et al., "Declining Prevalence of Anemia Among Low-Income Children in the United States," *Pediatrics* 258, no. 12 (1987): 1619–23; D. Rush, J. M. Alvir, D. A. Kenny, et al., "The National WIC Evaluation: Evaluation of the Special Supplemental Food Programs for Women, Infants and Children, IV: Study of Infants and Children," *American Journal of Clinical Nutrition* 48 (1988): 429–38. Lori Kowaleski-Jones and Greg Duncan, "Effects of Participation in the WIC Food Assistance Program on Children's Health and Development: Evidence from

NLSY Children," Discussion Paper no. 1207–00, Institute for Research on Poverty, 2000.

35. U.S. Centers for Disease Control. "Nutritional Status of Children Participating in the Special Supplemental Nutrition Program for Women, Infants, and Children—United States, 1988–1991," *Morbidity and Mortality Weekly* 45, no. 3 (1996): 65–69; Janet Currie and Marianne Bitler, "Medicaid at Birth, WIC Take-Up, and Children's Outcomes: A Final Report to the IRP/USDA Small Grants Program," May 2004.

36. Burstein, Fox, Hiller, Kornfeld, et al., "WIC General Analysis Project, Profile of WIC Children,"; Robert Pear, "Some Stores Cater to Poor But Bill U.S. for Top Prices," *New York Times*, June 6, 2004, p. 34.

37. Minnesota Budget Project, "Consequences: The Impact of Minnesota's Government Budget Cuts," Minnesota Council of NonProfits, Minneapolis, 2003. Idaho Central District Health Department, "WIC Informer," January/February/March 2004.

38. See the Food Research and Action Committee web page for further details about federal food programs: http://www.frac.org; see also *Federal Register* 68, no. 141, (July 23, 2003): 43487.

39. Physicians Committee for Responsible Medicine, "School Lunch Report Card," Washington, D.C., August 2003; Douglas Besharov, "We're Feeding the Poor As If They're Starving," *Washington Post*, December 8, 2002.

40. U.S. Department of Agriculture, Food and Nutrition Service, "School Nutrition Dietary Assessment Study—II, Final Report," CN-01-SNDAIIFR, Washington, D.C., April 2001.

41. Jean Tarbett, "Lunch Programs Face Scrutiny," *Herald Dispatch*, January 22, 2003.

42. Barbara Devaney, A. R. Gordon, and J. A. Burghardt," The School Nutrition Dietary Assessment Study: Dietary Intakes of Program Participants and Nonparticipants, U.S. Department of Agriculture, Food and Nutrition Service, Alexandria, Va., 1993.

43. Diane Whitmore, "Do School Lunches Contribute to Childhood Obesity?" mimeo, Harris School of Public Policy, University of Chicago, April 2005.

44. Bhattacharya and Currie, "Youths at Nutritional Risk."

45. Jayanta Bhattacharya, Janet Currie, and Steven Haider, "Breakfast of Champions? The Effects of the School Breakfast Program on Nutrition," NBER Working Paper, Cambridge, Mass. July 2004; Alan Myers, Amy E. Sampson, Michael Weitzman, et al., "School Breakfast Program

and School Performance," *American Journal of Diseases of Children* 143 (1989): 1234–39; J. M. Murphy, M. E. Pagano, J. Nachmani, P. Sperling, S. Kane, and R. E. Kleinman, "The Relationship of School Breakfast to Psychosocial and Academic Functioning: Cross-Sectional and Longitudinal Observations in an Inner-City School Sample," *Archives of Pediatric and Adolescent Medicine* 152, no. 9 (September 1998): 899–907.

46. Sandra Hofferth and Sally Curtin, "Do Food Programs Make Children Overweight?" Department of Family Studies, University of Maryland, College Park, Md., September 30, 2004.

47. U.S. Department of Agriculture, "Veneman Outlines Administration Goals for Child Nutrition Programs," news release no. 0073.03, Washington, D.C., February 25, 2003. Food Research and Action Center, "School Breakfast Scorecard: 2003," Washington, D.C., November 2003.

48. John Burghardt, Tim Silva, and Lara Hulsey, "Case Study of National School Lunch Program Verification Outcomes in Large Metropolitan School Districts," report no. CN-04-AV3, U.S. Department of Agriculture, Food and Nutrition Service, Alexandria, Va., April 2004; John Burghardt, Philip Gleason, Michael Sinclair, et al., "Evaluation of the National School Lunch Program Application/Verification Pilot Projects: Volume 1: Impacts on Deterrence, Barriers, and Accuracy," report no. CN-04-AV1, U.S. Department of Agriculture, Food and Nutrition Service, Alexandria, Va., February 2004; Zoe Neuberger and Robert Greenstein, "What Have We Learned from FNS' New Research Findings about Overcertification in the School Meals Programs?" Center on Budget and Policy Priorities, Washington, D.C., November 13, 2003; Rep. Miller quoted in Greg Toppo, "Free School Lunches May Face Audit," *USA Today*, January 16, 2003.

49. "Highlights of the Child Nutrition and WIC Reauthorization Act of 2004," Food Research and Action Center, Washington, D.C., September 13, 2004.

50. Kenneth Jackson, Phil Gleason, John Hall, and Rhonda Strauss, "Study of Direct Certification in the National School Lunch Program," report no. CN-00-DC, U.S. Department of Agriculture, Food and Nutrition Service, Alexandria, Va., September 2000; John Burghardt, Anne Gordon, Nancy Chapman, et al., "The School Nutrition Dietary Assessment Study: School Food Service, Meals Offered and Dietary Intake," U.S. Department of Agriculture, Food and Nutrition Service, Alexandria, Va., 1993.

51. Robert Moffitt and Thomas Fraker, "The Effect of Food Stamps on Labor Supply: A Bivariate Selection Model," *Journal of Public Economics* 35,

no. 1 (February 1988): 25–56; Robert A. Moffitt and Michael Keane, "A Structural Model of Multiple Welfare Program Participation and Labor Supply," *International Economic Review* 39, no. 3 (August 1998): 553–89; Paul Hagstrom, "The Food Stamp Participation and Labor Supply of Married Couples: An Empirical Analysis of Joint Decisions," *Journal of Human Resources* 31, no. 2 (spring 1996): 383–403.

52. Institute of Medicine of the National Academies, *WIC Food Packages: Time for a Change* (Washington, D.C.: National Academies Press, 2005).

Chapter 4

1. Gary Wisby, "Boy's Death Stunned City into Action," *Chicago Sun-Times*, February 9, 1994, p. 6; Leon Pitt, "Third Teen Guilty in Boy's Murder," *Chicago Sun-Times*, September 18, 1993, p. 5; National Public Radio, "Remorse: The 14 Stories of Eric Morse," 2004, available at http://www.npr.org/programs/morsetranscript.html.

2. U.S. General Accounting Office, "Public Housing: Converting to Housing Certificates Raises Major Questions About Cost," GAO/RCED-95-195, Washington, D.C., 1995.

3. The government also spends $1.6 billion per year on federal block grants to state and local governments for project-based aid (such as single-room occupancy buildings to serve the homeless) and provides assistance to low-income homeowners. For example, the Section 235 Program has subsidized about half a million households since 1969, while the Department of Agriculture's Section 502 Program has subsidized almost two million households since 1949.

4. "Section 515," "Section 236," and "Section 8 New or Substantial Rehabilitation" are all examples of this type of program. Edgar Olson provides an excellent overview of housing programs that assist renters; see "Housing Programs for Low-Income Households," in *Means Tested Transfer Programs in the United States*, ed. R. Moffitt; the Millennial Housing Commission ("Meeting Our Nation's Housing Challenges: Report of the Bipartisan Millennial Housing Commission Appointed by the Congress of the United States," Washington, D.C., 2002) offers a program-by-program description in appendix 3 of the report. See also Jennifer Oldham, "Housing for the Poor in the U.S. Faces Crisis," *Los Angeles Times*, June 23, 2001.

5. See http://www.lacdc.org/programs/improvements/guidelines.shtm.

6. Olson, "Housing Programs for Low-Income Households." Karen Gray works in Los Angeles helping nonprofits put together packages of LIHTC funds and other state and local subsidies so that they can build affordable housing.

7. Internal Revenue Service, "Low Income Housing Credit Newsletter," issue no. 2, February 2001.

8. It is very difficult to come up with accurate numbers about the number of people assisted by all programs because there are many different programs and some families are assisted by more than one program. Also, different publications take different approaches to categorizing the various smaller programs. The *Green Book* (which is produced by the Committee on Ways and Means to assist Congress in managing these programs) does not even have any estimates of the number of families assisted. A few comments on the appendix table 1 numbers (in this book): The *2004 Green Book* estimate of the total amount spent on Section 8 and other assisted rental housing does not include expenditures on LIHTC, which I have added in to yield 25.2. The number of households with tenant-based vouchers is not easy to come by, because HUD tends to report both project-based and tenant-based Section 8 expenditures together. The numbers for vouchers come from appendix 3 of the Millennial Housing Commission, while the total number of people assisted by Section 8 and other assisted rental housing is inferred from appendix 1, table 6 of that report, which says that about five million renter households are assisted (5 million less 1.3 million in projects is 3.7 million). Numbers on homeless programs, housing block grants (to states), and USDA rural programs were produced by the author summing the amounts listed for various programs in pages K10–K12 of the *2004 Green Book*.

Olson, "Housing Programs for Low-Income Households," table 5. Some families both live in projects financed under Section 515 or Section 236 and receive assistance from Section 8, and so the total number of households assisted is about 235,650 less than the sum of the numbers given here.

9. New York City Housing Authority, "Factsheet," April 19, 2004, available at http://www.nyc.gov/html/nycha/html/factshett.html; Los Angeles County Community Development Commission, "How to Apply for Public Housing," available at http://www.lacdc.org/housing/apply_public/apply.shtm; Boston Housing Authority, "Housing Services," available at http://www.bostonhousing.org/housgin_services.html; Philadelphia Housing Authority, "How to Apply for Public Housing," 2004, available at

http://www.pha.phila.gov/housing/admis-default.aspx; Fred Guarino. "Public Housing Closes Some Waiting Lists," *Shelby County Reporter*, June 1, 2004; Chicago Housing Authority, "A Voice for Change," 2003, available at http://www.thecha.org/; Housing Link, "Waiting List Status Report," 2004, available at http://www.housinglink.org/WLSR.htm/.

10. U.S. Department of Housing and Urban Development, "Characteristics of HUD-Assisted Renters and Their Units in 1989," Washington, D.C., 1992, table 1–1.

11. Kathryn Nelson, Mark Treskon, and Danilo Pelletiere, "Losing Ground in the Best of Times: Low Income Renters in the 1990s," National Low Income Housing Coalition, Washington, D.C., March 2004.

12. See U.S. Department of Housing and Urban Development, "Housing in the Seventies," Washington, D.C., 1974; Stephen Mayo, Shirley Mansfield, David Warner, and Richard Zwetchkenbaum, "Housing Allowances and Other Rental Assistance Programs—A Comparison Based on the Housing Allowance Demand Experiment Part 2: Costs and Efficiency," Abt Associates, Cambridge, Mass., June 1980; Edgar Olsen and David Baron, "The Benefits and Costs of Public Housing in New York City," *Journal of Public Economics* 20 (April 1983): 299–332; James Wallace, Susan Bloom, William Holshouser, Shirley Mansfield, and Daniel Weinberg, "Participation and Benefits in the Urban Section 8 Program: New Construction and Existing Housing," vols. 1 and 2, Abt Associates, Cambridge, Mass., January 1981; Ann Schnare, Carla Pendone, William Moss, and Kathleen Heintz, "The Costs of HUD Multifamily Housing Programs: A Comparison of the Development, Financing and Life Cycle Costs of Section 8, Public Housing, and Other Major HUD Programs," vols. 1 and 2, Urban Systems Research and Engineering, Cambridge, Mass., May 1982; U.S. General Accounting Office "Federal Housing Programs: What They Cost and What They Provide," GAO-01–901R, Washington, D.C., July 18, 2001; the Center on Budget and Policy Priorities ("Section 8 Utilization and the Proposed Housing Voucher Success Fund," March 22, 2000) argues that the poorest families cannot afford to live in LIHTC units unless they also receive vouchers.

13. Olson, "Housing Programs for Low-Income Households."

14. A very low-income person is defined as one with income less than 50 percent of the area median income for purposes of housing policy. See U.S. Department of Housing and Urban Development, "Rental Housing Assistance. The Crisis Continues: The 1997 Report to Congress on Worst Case Housing Needs," Washington, D.C., 1998.

15. See note 10.

16. Bhattacharya, Currie, Haider, and DeLeire, "Heat or Eat?"

17. It is possible, however, that these outcomes reflect other problems that these families have, such as high rates of parental drug abuse and domestic violence. See David Wood, Burciaga Valdez, Toshi Hayashi, and Albert Shen, "Health of Homeless Children and Housed, Poor Children," *Pediatrics* 86, no. 6 (December 1990): 858–66.

18. William Julius Wilson, *The Truly Disadvantaged: Crime and Family Disruption in U.S. Cities* (Chicago: University of Chicago Press, 1997). On spacial mismatch, David Ellwood argues that black and white teens living in the same neighborhood have dramatically different unemployment rates; see "The Spacial Mismatch Hypothesis: Are There Jobs Missing in the Ghetto?" in *The Black Youth Employment Crisis*, edited by Richard Freeman and Harry Holzer (Chicago: University of Chicago Press, 1986). More recent work by Michael Stolls and Steven Raphael finds that blacks are more segregated from their jobs than others: See "Modest Progress: The Narrowing Spatial Mismatch Between Blacks and Jobs in the 1990s," Brookings Institution, Washington, D.C., December 2002. See also Susan Mayer and Christopher Jencks, "The Social Consequences of Growing Up in a Poor Neighborhood," in *Inner-City Poverty in the United States*, edited by Laurence Lynn and Michael McGeary (Washington, D.C.: National Academy Press, 1990).

19. See Kenneth Jackson, "Federal Subsidy and the American Dream," in *Crabgrass Frontier: The Suburbanization of the United States* (New York: Oxford University Press, 1985); Robert Schafer and Helen Ladd, *Discrimination in Mortgage Lending* (Cambridge: MIT Press, 1981).

20. Nicholas Lemann, *The Promised Land: The Great Black Migration and How It Changed America* (New York: Knopf, 1991).

21. Douglas Massey and Nancy Denton, *American Apartheid: Segregation and the Making of the Underclass* (Cambridge: Harvard University Press, 1993).

22. Michael Murray, "Subsidized and Unsubsidized Housing Starts: 1961–1977," *Review of Economics and Statistics* 65 (November 1983): 590–97; Murray, "Subsidized and Unsubsidized Housing Stocks 1935 to 1987: Crowding Out and Cointegration," *Journal of Real Estate Economics and Finance* 19 (1999): 107–204; Edgar Olsen, "Fundamental Housing Policy Reform," manuscript, Department of Economics, University of Virginia, Charlottesville, Va., November 2003.

23. Edgar Olson. "The Millennial Housing Commission Report: An Assessment," AREUEA mid-year meeting, May 28, 2003.

24. The key is to compare the project children with other similar children. To do this, we use the fact that families with boys and girls are entitled to larger public housing units and are more likely to participate than families with same-sex children. Hence, we compare families that are similar except for the fact that they happen to have children of different sex. See Janet Currie and Aaron Yelowitz, "Are Public Housing Projects Good For Kids?" *Journal of Public Economics* 75, no. 1 (January 2000): 99–124.

25. Brian Jacob, "Public Housing, Housing Vouchers and Student Achievement: Evidence from Public Housing Demolitions in Chicago," *American Economics Review* 94, no. 1 (March 2004): 233–58.

26. Raymond Struyk and Marc Bendick, eds., *Housing Vouchers for the Poor: Lessons from a National Experiment* (Washington, D.C.: Urban Institute, 1981).

27. Susan Popkïn and Mary Cunningham, *CHAC Section 8 Programs: Barriers to Successful Leasing Up* (Washington, D.C.: Urban Institute, 1999); Popkin and Cunningham, *Searching for Rental Housing with Section 8 in the Chicago Region* (Washington, D.C.: Urban Institute, 2000); Elizabeth Mulroy, "The Search for Affordable Housing," in *Women as Single Parents: Confronting the Institutional Barriers in the Courts, the Workplace and the Housing Market*, ed. Elizabeth Mulroy (New York: Auburn House, 1988).

28. James Rosenbaum, L. S. Rubinowitz, and M. J. Kulieke, "Low Income African-American Children in White Suburban Schools," Center for Urban Affairs and Policy Research, Northwestern University, Evanston, Ill., 1986; James Rosenbaum, "Black Pioneers—Do Their Moves to the Suburbs Increase Economic Opportunity for Mothers and Children?" *Housing Policy Debate* 2, no. 4 (1992): 1179–213; James Rosenbaum, "Changing the Geography of Opportunity by Expanding Residential Choice: Lessons from the Gautreaux Program," *Housing Policy Debate* 6, no. 1 (1995): 231–69.

29. Larry Orr, Judith Feins, Robin Jacob, Eric Beecroft, Lisa Sanbonmatsu, Lawrence Katz, Jeffrey Liebman, and Jeffrey Kling, "Moving to Opportunity: Interim Impacts Evaluation," U.S. Department of Housing and Urban Development, Washington, D.C., 2003.

30. Philip Oreopoulos, "The Long-Run Consequences of Living in a Poor Neighborhood," *Quarterly Journal of Economics* 118, no. 4 (November 2003): 1533–75.

31. Carlos Jackson, "Testimony of Carlos Jackson, Executive Director, Los Angeles County Community Development Commission and Housing

Authority of the County of Los Angeles, before the House Financial Services Subcommittee on Housing and Community Oportunity," July 1, 2003; Abt Associates, "Section 8 Rental Voucher and Rental Certificate Utilization Study," U.S. Department of Housing and Urban Development Washington, D.C., October 1994. This latter study did not include data from Los Angeles, but it found that outside of New York City, 87 percent of searchers were able to find housing. In New York City the rate was 62 percent.

32. Stephen Kennedy and Meryl Finkel, "Section 8 Rental Voucher and Rental Certificate Utilization Study," Abt Associates, Cambridge, Mass., 1994.

33. Amy Crews Cutts and Edgar Olsen, "Are Section 8 Housing Subsidies Too High?" *Journal of Housing Economics* 11 (2002): 214–43.

34. Peter Rydell, Kevin Neels, and Lance Barnett, "Price Effects of a Housing Allowance Program," RAND report no. R-2720-HUD, Santa Monica, Calif., September 1982.

35. Dirk Early and Edgar Olsen, "Subsidized Housing, Emergency Shelters, and Homelessness: An Empirical Investigation Using Data from the 1990 Census," *Advances in Economics Analysis and Policy* 2 (2002): 1–34.

36. Christopher Jencks, *The Homeless* (Cambridge: Harvard University Press, 1994); Martha Burt and Laudan Aron, *Helping America's Homeless* (Washington, D.C.: Urban Institute, 2001).

37. Lynette Holloway, "With a New Look and Purpose, S.R.O.'s Make a Comeback," *New York Times*, November 10, 1996; Sam Tsemberis and Ronda Eisenberg, "Pathways to Housing: Supported Housing for Street-Dwelling Homeless Individuals with Psychiatric Disabilities," *Psychiatric Services* 51 (April 2000): 487, 493. According to Tsemberis and Eisenberg, traditional approaches to the problem of homelessness among the mentally ill emphasize compliance with treatment protocols. Only compliant clients are eligible for housing. In contrast, the Pathways program first tries to get people into housing of their choice, and then offers treatment services.

38. Gavin Newsom quoted in "Going Places: An Ambitious Young Mayor Takes San Franciso," *New Yorker*, October 4, 2004, p. 46.

39. Cutts and Olsen, "Are Section 8 Housing Subsides Too High?"

40. National Low Income Housing Coalition, "Changing Priorities: The Federal Budget and Housing Assistance 1996–2006," 2001.

41. U.S. House of Representatives, Committee on Ways and Means, *2004 Green Book*.

Chapter 5

1. See David Crary, "The Childcare Money Gap," *Associated Press*, Nashville, Tenn., October 20, 2003.

2. National Research Council and Institute of Medicine, *Working Families and Growing Kids*.

3. David Blau and Janet Currie. "Who's Minding the Kids? Preschool, Day Care, and After School Care," in *The Handbook of Education Economics*, edited by Finis Welch and Eric Hanushek (New York: North Holland, forthcoming); K. M. Dwyer, J. L. Richardon, K. L. Daley, et al., "Characteristics of Eight Grade Students Who Initiate Self Care in Elementary and Junior High School," *Pediatrics* 86 (1990); Anna Aizer, "Home Alone: Child Care and the Behavior of School-Age Children," *Journal of Public Economics* 88, nos. 9–10 (2004): 1835–48; U.S. Office of Juvenile Justice and Delinquency Prevention, "Juvenile Offenders and Victims: A National Report," Washington, D.C., 1996.

4. This literature is summarized in Blau and Currie, "Who's Minding the Kids?" See also National Research Council and Institute of Medicine, *Working Families and Growing Kids*.

5. U.S. House of Representatives, Committee on Ways and Means, *Overview of Entitlement Programs: 1994 Green Book* (Washington, D.C.: U.S. Government Printing Office, 1994).

6. U.S. House of Representatives, Committee on Ways and Means, 2004, tables 9–12.

7. Most figures in this paragraph come from U.S. House of Representatives, Committee on Ways and Means, *2004 Green Book*. States are supposed to set their subsidy rate at the 75th percentile of the fee that they obtain using a local market survey. For a discussion of rate setting, see Gina Adam, J. Sandefort, and Nancy Ebb, "Locked Doors: States Struggling to Meet the Child Care Needs of Low-Income Working Families," Children's Defense Fund, Washington, D.C., 1998.

8. Karen Schulman and Helen Blank, "Child Care Assistance Policies 2001–2004: Families Struggling to Move Forward, States Going Backward," issue brief, National Women's Law Center, Washington, D.C., September 2004.

9. Brian Riedl, "Six Myths About Child Care," Backgrounder no. 1588, Heritage Foundation, Washington, D.C., September 19, 2002.

10. Bruce Fuller, Sharon L. Kagan, Jan McCarthy, Gretchen Caspary, Darren Lubotsky, and Laura Gascue, "Who Selects Formal Child Care?

The Role of Subsidies as Low-Income Mothers Negotiate Welfare Reform," presented at the Society for Research in Child Development Meeting, Albuquerque, N.M., April 1999.

11. Bong Joo Lee, Robert Goerge, Mairead Reidy, J. Lee Kreader, Annie Georges, Robert L. Wagmiller, Jr., Jane Staveley, David Stevens, and Ann Dryden Witte, "Child Care Subsidy Use and Employment Outcomes of Low-Income Mothers during Early Years of Welfare Reform: A Three-State Study," Chapin Hall Center for the Study of Children, University of Chicago, 2004.

12. Anne Witte and Magaly Queralt, "Take-Up Rates and Trade-Offs after the Age of Entitlement: Some Thoughts and Empirical Evidence for Child Care Subsidies," NBER Working Paper no. 8886, Cambridge, Mass., April 2002.

13. Marcia Meyers and Theresa Heintze, "The Performance of the Child Care Subsidy System: Target Efficiency, Coverage Adequacy and Equity," *Social Service Review* 73, no. 1 (March 1999): 37–64.

14. Gina Adams, Kathleen Snyder, and Jodi Sandfort, 2002. "Getting and Retaining Child Care Assistance: How Policy and Practice Influence Parents? Experiences," Occasional Paper no. 55. Urban Institute, Washington, D.C.; Gina Adams and Monica Rohacek, "Child Care and Welfare Reform, Welfare Reform and Beyond Brief no. 14, Brookings Institution, Washington, D.C., February 2002.

15. Mark Berger and Dan Black, "Child Care Subsidies, Quality of Care, and the Labor Supply of Low-Income Single Mothers," *Review of Economics and Statistics* 74, no. 4 (1992): 635–42; Jonah Gelbach, "Public Schooling for Young Children and Maternal Labor Supply," *American Economic Review* 92, no.1 (March 2002): 307–22.

16. Erdal Tekin, "Working at Night: Standard Work, Child Care Subsidies, and Lessons for Welfare Reform," NBER Working Paper no. 10274, Cambridge, Mass., February 2004.

17. David Blau ("Unintended Consequences of Child Care Regulations," manuscript, University of North Carolina, Chapel Hill, 2003) discusses lax enforcement of child-care regulation. See also Naci Mocan, "Quality Adjusted Cost Functions for Child Care Centers," *American Economic Review Papers and Proceedings* 85, no. 2 (1995): 409–13.

18. U.S. House of Representatives, Committee on Ways and Means, *2004 Green Book*; see table 9–21.

19. Jim Hopkins and Michael Quinlan, "Series: Early Childhood: A Growing Concern; Kentucky Child-Care Standards Don't Aim High,"

Courier Journal, December 7, 1999; KY., Bob Reynolds, "Day Care Center Called Dangerous Closed," WNEP Newswatch 16, September 7, 2004, available at http://www.wnep.com.

20. Jim Hoffer, "Dangerous Blind Spots Found in Day Care Oversight," WABC-TV New York, Eye Witness News, October 14, 2004.

21. John M. Love, Peter Z. Schochet, and Alicia L. Meckstroth, "Are They in Any Real Danger? What Research Does—and Doesn't Tell Us about Child Care Quality and Children's Well-Being," Mathematica Policy Research, Princeton, N.J., May 1996, p. 5.

22. Susan Helburn and Carollee Howes, "Child Care Cost and Quality," *The Future of Children* 6, no. 2 (1996): 62–82. I am quoting Deborah Lowe Vandell of the University of Wisconsin.

23. These studies include the "Cost, Quality, and Outcomes Study" (CQOS) and the "National Child Care Staffing Study" (NCCSS), which measured quality using the Early Childhood Environment Rating Scale (ECERS) and its infant-toddler counterpart (ITERS). These instruments rate each observed classroom on thirty to thirty-five items, using a scale of 1–7 for each item. For further discussion, see Blau and Currie, "Who's Minding the Kids?"

24. Blau and Currie ("Who's Minding the Kids?") summarize several studies showing that stronger regulation "crowds" people out of regulated care.

25. Naci Mocan, "Can Consumers Detect Lemons? Information Asymmetry in the Market for Child Care," NBER Working Paper no. 8291, Cambridge, Mass., May.2001; James Walker, "Public Policy and the Supply of Child Care Services," in *The Economics of Child Care*, ed. David Blau (New York: Russell Sage Foundation, 1991); Deborah Cryer and Margaret Burchinal, "Parents as Child Care Consumers," in "Cost, Quality, and Child Outcomes in Child Care Centers, Technical Report," ed. Suzanne W. Helburn, Department of Economics, Center for Research in Economic and Social Policy, University of Colorado, Denver, June 1995, pp. 203–20.

26. David Blau and Janet Currie ("Who's Minding the Kids") offer a summary of this literature. The study discussed here is "NICHD Early Child Care Research Network"; see also Greg J. Duncan, "Modeling the Impacts of Child Care Quality on Children's Preschool Cognitive Development," *Child Development* 74, no. 5 (October 2003): 1454–75. Technically, the paper found that a two standard deviation change in child-care

quality was associated with a one-sixth to one-seventh standard deviation in cognitive test scores. Under certain assumptions about the distribution of quality, a two standard deviation change is about the distance between care of middle quality and worst-quality care. A problem with the NICHD study is that all of the research is jointly authored by a consortium of academics, and so it is taking a long time for results to be made public.

27. Jack Shonkoff, Deborah Phillips, and Bonnie Keilty, eds., *Early Childhood Intervention: Views from the Field, Shonkoff, National Research Council and Institutes of Medicine* (Washington, D.C.: National Academy Press, 2000); James J. Heckman and Yona Rubenstein, "The Importance of Noncognitive Skills: Lessons from the GED Testing Program," *American Economic Review* 91, no. 2 (May 2001): 145–49; Valerie Lee, Jeanne Brooks-Gunn, E. Schnur, and F. R. Liaw, "Are Head Start Effects Sustained? A Longitudinal Follow-up Comparison of Disadvantaged Children Attending Head Start, No Preschool, and Other Preschool Programs," *Child Development* 61 (1990): 495–507.

28. While randomized trials are the "gold standard" for evidence in many fields, they are not without their own problems. James Heckman and Jeffrey Smith discuss many of the potential pitfalls in "Assessing the Case for Social Experiments," *Journal of Economic Perspectives* 9, no. 2 (Spring 1995): 85–110.

29. Frances Campbell and Craig T. Ramey, "Effects of Early Intervention on Intellectual and Academic Achievement: A Follow-up Study of Children from Low-Income Families," *Child Development* 65 (1994): 684–698; Frances Campbell and Craig T. Ramey, "Cognitive and School Outcomes for High-Risk African-American Students at Middle Adolescence: Positive Effects of Early Intervention," *American Educational Research Journal* 32, no. 4 (1995): 743–72; Leonard Masse and W. Steven Barnett, "A Benefit Cost Analysis of the Abecedarian Early Childhood Intervention," National Institute for Early Education Research, Rutgers University, New Brunswick, N.J., 2002.

30. Lawrence Schweinhart, Helen Barnes, and David Weikart, "*Significant Benefits: The High/Scope Perry Preschool Study Through Age 27,*" monograph no. 10 (Ypsilanti, Mich.: High-Scope Educational Research Foundation, 1993. For a more in-depth discussion of cost-benefit calculations, see Lynn Karoly et al., *Investing in Our Children: What We Know and Don't Know About the Costs and Benefits of Early Childhood Interventions* (Santa Monica, Calif.: RAND, 1998).

31. For cost numbers, see Blau and Currie, "Who's Minding the Kids." See also Edward Zigler and Sally J. Styfco, "Head Start: Criticisms in a Constructive Context," *American Psychologist* 49, no. 2 (February 1994): 127–32; Gary Resnick and Nicholas Zill, "Is Head Start Providing High-Quality Educational Services? Unpacking Classroom Processes," mimeo, Westat, n.d.

32. Janet Currie and Matthew Neidell, "Getting Inside the Black Box of Head Start Program Quality: What Matters and What Doesn't," manuscript, Department of Economics, UCLA, September 2004.

33. Deanne Smith and Dan Margolies, "Head Start Fallout Spreads: Congress Notices KC Director's Salary," *Kansas City Star*, October 18, 2003.

34. U.S. House of Representatives, Committee on Education and the Workforce, "New HHS Report Offers Mixed Results on Accountability in Head Start, Raises New Questions," May 13, 2004.

35. John Hendren, "U.S. Pacific Command Nominee Bows Out: Air Force General Withdraws after McCain Grills Him over Boeing Tanker Deal at Hearing," *Los Angeles Times*, October 7, 2004.

36. For criticism of Head Start see, for example, John Hood, "Caveat Emptor: The Head Start Scam," Cato Institute Washington, D.C., December 18, 1992. For a description of the evaluation experiment and early results, see U.S. Department of Health and Human Services, "Head Start Impact Study First Year Findings," Washington, D.C., June 2005.

37. Janet Currie and Duncan Thomas, "Does Head Start Make a Difference?" *American Economic Review* 85, no. 3 (1995): 341–64; Currie and Thomas, "Does Head Start Help Hispanic Children?" *Journal of Public Economics* 74, no. 2 (1999): 235–62.

38. Janet Currie and Duncan Thomas, "School Quality and the Longer-Term Effects of Head Start," *Journal of Human Resources* 35, no. 4 (2000): 755–74; Valerie Lee and Susanna Loeb, "Where Do Head Start Attendees End Up? One Reason Why Preschool Effects Fade Out," *Educational Evaluation and Policy Analysis* 17, no. 1 (1995): 62–82.

39. Sherri Oden, Lawrence Schweinhart, and David Weikart, *Into Adulthood: A Study of the Effects of Head Start* (Ypsilanti, Mich.: High/Scope Press, 2000).

40. A possible problem is that the Head Start questions refer to events that took place many years ago. Yet the Head Start enrollment rates implied by the PSID match well with administrative data. See Eliana Garces,

Duncan Thomas, and Janet Currie, "Longer-Term Effects of Head Start," *American Economic Review* 92, no. 4 (2002): 999–1012.

41. See Currie and Neidell, "Getting Inside the Black Box."

42. Martha Buell, Ilka Pfister, and Michael Gamel-McCormick, "Caring for the Caregiver: Early Head Start/Family Child Care Partnerships," *Infant Mental Health Journal* 23, nos. 1–2 (2002): 213–30; Diane Paulsell, Ellen Eliason Kisker, John M. Love, and Helen Raikes, "Understanding Implementation in Early Head Start Programs: Implications for Policy and Practice," *Infant Mental Health Journal* 23, nos. 1–2 (2002): 14–35; Helen Raikes and John M. Love, "Early Head Start: A Dynamic New Program for Infants and Toddlers and Their Families," *Infant Mental Health Journal* 23, nos. 1–2 (2002): 1–13.

43. Georgia established a universal voluntary program for four-year-olds in 1995. New York followed in 1997, and Oklahoma expanded an existing program serving disadvantaged kids into a universal four-year-old program in 1998. In New York, only 200 out of 700 school districts were participating in 2002, and the continued existence of the program is in jeopardy due to budget crises. For a discussion of evaluation efforts, see Walter Gilliam and Edward Zigler, "A Critical Meta-analysis of All Evaluations of State-Funded Preschool from 1977 to 1998: Implications for Policy, Service Delivery, and Program Evaluation, *Early Childhood Research Quarterly* no. 4 (2001): 441–73; Katherine Magnuson, Christopher Ruhm, and Jane Waldfogel, "Does Prekindergarten Improve School Preparation and Performance?" NBER Working Paper no. 10452, Cambridge, Mass., April 2004.

44. Michael Baker, Jonathan Gruber, and Kevin Milligan, "Universal Child Care, Maternal Labor Supply, and Child Well-Being," working paper, July 2005.

45. Robert Schwanebert, "Preschool Program's Cost Lands in Court," *Star-Ledger*, Newark, N.J., October 25, 2004.

46. See Carla Rivera, "Reviewers Taking a Studied Look at County Preschools," *Los Angeles Times*, March 14, 2005, p. B1.

47. California Secretary of State, "California General Election Official Voter Information Guide," Sacramento, Calif., fall 2002.

48. P. S. Seppanen, J. M. Love, D. K. deVries, L. Bernstein, M. Seligson, F. Marx, and E. E. Kisker, "National Study of Before- and After-School Programs," U.S. Department of Education, Washington, D.C., 1993; National Research Council and Institute of Medicine, *Working Families and Growing Kids*.

49. Pauline Brooks, Cynthia M. Mojica, and Robert E. Land, "Final Evaluation Report. Longitudinal Study of LA's BEST After-School Education and Enrichment Program," mimeo, UCLA Center for the Study of Evaluation, Graduate School of Education and Information Studies, 1995; Denise Huang, Barry Gribbons, Kyung Sung Kim, Charlotte Lee, and Eva L. Baker, "A Decade of Results: The Impact of LA's BEST After-School Enrichment Program on Subsequent Student Achievement and Performance," Mimeo, UCLA Center for the Study of Evaluation, Graduate School of Education and Information Studies, 2000; Denise Huang, Denise, Shu-jiao Lin, and Tina Henderson, "Evaluating the Impact of LA's BEST on Students' Social and Academic Development: Study of 74 LA's BEST Sites 2001–2002 Phase I Preliminary Report," Mimeo, UCLA Center for the Study of Evaluation, Graduate School of Education and Information Studies, 2001; Darrell Morris, Beverly Shaw, and Jan Penney, "Helping Low Readers in Grades 2 and 3: An After-School Volunteer Tutoring Program," *The Elementary School Journal*, 91, no. 2 (1990): 133–50; Los Angeles Unified School District, "Rapid Gains Reflected in 2000–2001 Stanford 9 Results," Office of Communications News Release, August 14, 2001. For a more detailed summary of these results, see Blau and Currie, "Who's Minding the Kids?"

50. A. Hahn, T. Leavitt, and P. Aaron, "Evaluation of the Quantum Opportunities Program. Did the Program Work? A Report on the Postsecondary Outcomes and Cost-Effectiveness of the QOP 1989–1993," Brandeis University Heller Graduate School Center for Human Resources, Waltham, Mass., 1994; J. P. Tiernay, Jean Baldwin Grossman, and N. Resch, "Making a Difference: An Impact Study of Big Brothers/Big Sisters," Public/Private Ventures, Philadelphia, Pa., 1995; Joseph Kahne and Kim Bailey, "The Role of Social Capital in Youth Development: The Case of 'I Have a Dream' Programs," *Educational Evaluation and Policy Analysis* 21, no. 3 (1999): 321–43.

51. A recent RAND study offers a particularly scathing overview of the available research. See Susan Bodilly and Megan Beckett, *Making Out-of-School Time Matter* (Santa Monica, Calif.: RAND, 2005).

52. Mark Dynarski, Susanne James-Burdumy, Mary Moore, Linda Rosenberg, John Deke, and Wendy Mansfield, *When Schools Stay Open Late: The National Evaluation of the 21st Century Community Learning Centers Program* (Washington, D.C.: U.S. Department of Education National Center for Education Evaluation and Regional Assistance, 2004).

53. James Heckman, "Policies to Foster Human Capital," *Research in Labor Economics* 54, no. 1 (March 2000).

Chapter 6

1. Milton Friedman, *Capitalism and Freedom*, (Chicago: University of Chicago Press, 1962), 190.

2. Robert Moffitt, "Incentive Effects of the U.S. Welfare System," *Journal of Economic Literature* 30 (March 1992): 1–62.

3. See U.S. House of Representatives, Committe on Ways and Means, *2000 Green Book* (Washington, D.C.: U.S. Government Printing Office, 2000), tables 15.34 and 15.35. The cutbacks to the school nutrition programs were contained in the Omnibus Budget Reconciliation Act of 1981. P.L. 99–500 and P.L. 99–661 increased reimbursements for school meals and made it easier for families to enroll by providing for automatic eligibility of children whose families received food stamps or AFDC.

4. Leighton Ku, "CDC Data Show Medicaid and SCHIP Played a Critical Counter-Cyclical Role in Strengthening Health Insurance Coverage During the Economic Downturn," Center on Budget and Policy Priorities, Washington, D.C., October 8, 2003.

5. U.S. Census Bureau, "Poverty Status of People, by Age, Race, and Hispanic Origin: 1959 to 2001," available at http://www.census.gov/income/histpov/hstpov3.lst.

6. Center on Budget and Policy Priorities, "Strengths of the Safety Net: How the EITC, Social Security, and Other Government Programs Affect Poverty," Center on Budget and Policy Priorities Research Report 98–020, March 1998.

7. Connie F. Citro and Robert T. Michael, eds., *Measuring Poverty: A New Approach* (Washington, D.C.: National Academy Press, 1995), John Iceland, Kathleen Short, Thesia Garner, and David Johnson, "Are Children Worse Off? Evaluating Child Well-Being Using a New (and Improved) Measure of Poverty," U.S. Census Bureau, Poverty Measurement Working Paper, April 1999.

8. Amy Goldstein, "Medicaid Plan Gives More Say to States: Bush Seeks to Alter Health Care for Poor," *Washington Post*, February 1, 2003, p. A01.

9. Danna Harmon. "The Struggle to Pay Rent Is about to Get Harder," *Christian Science Monitor*, May 12, 2004.

10. "Killing Off Housing for the Poor," *New York Times*, editorial, May 10, 2004.

11. Rachel Schumacher, "The Long and Winding Road: Head Start Reauthorization So Far," Center for Law and Social Policy, Washington, D.C., January 15, 2004.

12. Jackson, "Testimony of Carlos Jackson."

13. Ku and Nimalendran, "Losing Out: States are Cutting 1.2 to 1.6 Million Low-Income People from Medicaid, SCHIP and Other State Health Insurance Programs"; Elizabeth McNichol and Madeda Harris, "Many States Cut Budgets as Fiscal Squeeze Continues," Center on Budget and Policy Priorities, Washington D.C., April 26, 2004; Robin Toner and Robert Pear, "Cutbacks Imperil Health Coverage for States' Poor," *New York Times*, April 28, 2003, p. A1; Polly Ross Hughes, "Rule Changes Push Thousands of Children off Insurance Rolls," *Houston Chronicle*, November 12, 2003.

14. One of the best-known studies on this topic is Timothy Besley and Anne Case, "Incumbent Behavior: Vote-Seeking, Tax Setting, and Yardstick Competition," *American Economic Review* (March 1995): 25–45; see also Katherine Baicker, "Extensive or Intensive Generosity? The Price and Income Effects of Federal Grants," *Review of Economics and Statistics* 87, no. 2 (2005): 371–84.

15. William Gale and Laurence Kotlikoff, "Effects of Recent Fiscal Policies on Today's Children and Future Generations," Brookings Insitution, Washington D.C., May 21, 2004; Kaiser Family Foundation, "Medicaid: The Medicare Prescription Drug Law Fact Sheet," March 2004.

16. Robert Greenstein, Richard Kogan, and Joel Friedman, "Budget Priorities under the Senate Budget Plan," Center on Budget and Policy Priorities, Washington, D.C., April 2, 2004.

17. John Isaacs, "Current Status of Missile Defense Program," Center for Arms Control and Non-Proliferation, Washington, D.C., May 2004; Brian Riedl, "The Cost of America's Farm Subsidy Binge: An Average of $1 Million Per Farm," Heritage Foundation, Washington, D.C., December 10, 2001; Kenneth Harney, "Homeowner Subsidies Top $100 Billion Yearly," *Real Estate News and Advice*, May 17, 2004.

18. Warren Vieth, "Senate Passes Big Tax Breaks," *Los Angeles Times*, October 12, 2004, p. 1.

19. Besharov, "We're Feeding the Poor as If They're Starving."

20. As of July 2003, there were 73 million children zero to seventeen in the United States, according to the U.S. Census Bureau. The estimate is derived by summing the expenditures for non-cash programs shown in table 1 in the appendix and dividing by the total number of children. In

making this calculation, I assumed that only half of food stamp expenditures and two-thirds of housing assistance was for households with children.

21. House Ways and Means Chairman Bill Thomas has suggested that this provision be included in Social Security legislation (see Jonathan Weisman, "Automatic Signup in 401(k)s Backed," *Washington Post*, May 22, 2005, p. A5).

Index